CONTENTS

When I Was Young	1
Introduction	2
Chapter 1 – Excuses	6
Chapter 2 - Growing Up	25
Chapter 3 – Education	81
Chapter 4 – Motoring	84
Chapter 5 – Working	103
Chapter 6 – Working abroad	108
Chapter 7 – Sport	114
Chapter 8 - Marriage	165
Chapter 9 – Food	180
Chapter 10 - Shorts	183

WHEN I WAS YOUNG

INTRODUCTION

How did all this start?

In September 2020 we were coming to the end of our first release from lock down due to the COVID 19 pandemic. Twenty four senior golfers from Willingdon GC managed to get away on their annual golf trip, in this case to the Dorset Golf and Country Club at Bere Regis, Dorset. As a result of one alcohol fuelled evening full of fascinating stories I, naively stated that we should record these stories for posterity, as I thought they were part of social history and, somewhat impetuously, I promised to collate it. I am not sure on the following morning how many of those who were party to the discussion actually remembered my commitment. Now I think of it I could probably have walked away then. However I persisted and the end result was a book entitled 'What's Your Story?'* comprising of some 100 stories from 30 contributors. I suppose, in local terms the book was a relative success and went on to sell some 85 books and to raise, at the time of writing, £535 for the 2021 Senior Captains charity, Demelza Children's Hospice.

So, why produce this book, 'When I Was Young'? In December 2021 I was playing a round of golf at Willingdon with two others, who shall be nameless, Ha-ha. Roger was not having a good day. On the 16th Tee he made yet another excuse for a bad tee shot when our third colleague Tim said, "Mel, have you ever heard so many excuses from one person?" Ping! A light bulb moment! "'What's Your Excuse?' sounds like a good title for a book." Say I, and so the process began.

Unfortunately, it turns out that not many people are good at confessing to excuses, at least not the elaborately constructed ones that would fill a book. I received lots of short ones which regrettably would not even have filled a pamphlet let alone a book. So after a couple of months of trying to extract blood from stone and a discussion with the guys who inspired the original book I decided to change tack and widen the contributions to 'When I was Young'. What we now have is an insight into a way of life from the 1940s to the turn of the century, a world that seems light years away from that of today. It is often said that those born between 1940 and 1970 were the 'Golden Generation'. We had it easy, no world wars, no stress, no anxiety, in general a peaceful period of continuous growth. Maybe some of these stories will contradict that image of Nirvana, and show that we had little to keep us entertained, had to work hard to benefit from improved standards of living and generally make the most of what we had. You will find some stories, some anecdotes and some memories of what life was like growing up in the latter half of the 20th century. Most stories are printed as they were sent to me with only minor amendments to punctuation and grammar.

As the original idea was 'What's Your Excuse' I have used these stories to form the first chapter. You may also notice the theme 'Eating in the 1950s' running through the book. I trust this will spark a few memories. I hope you enjoy the read.

*All proceeds will go to the charity of the senior captain in post at the time of purchase. * 'What's Your Story?' is still available on Amazon Kindle Books. For those who wish to purchase a good read type: Mel Lockett – What's Your Story? into the Kindle books search box. I promise you will enjoy it whilst at the same time supporting a worthy*

MR MEL LOCKETT

charity.

Mel Lockett

Acknowledgements

It would be remiss of me not to acknowledge the contributors to this book. Quite often acknowledgements are placed at the back of a book which to me suggests they are an afterthought. Well, not in this case as without them there would be no book. My heartfelt thanks go to all those who have encouraged me but specifically those brave souls who were prepared to put pen to paper, fingers to keyboard, iPad, tablet or email, search deep into the recesses of their memories, and then finally stick their heads above the parapet and send me a contribution. Thank you.

In alphabetical order: Barry Alford, Adrian Beal, Hugh Ball, Perry Begin, John Bottomley, Dave Burnett, Reg Cork, John Court, Alan Elms, Jim Fell, Tim Franklin, Ray Fry, Mike Hartley, John Heald, Richard Holste, Geoff Long, John Maynard, Nigel Parkes, Bill Prest, Paul Roberts, Malcolm Robertson, Malcolm Rolfe, Roger Savage, Graham Shaw, Bob Smith, Peter Smith, Richard Stone, Tony Uden, Roger Vaughn, Mike Williams and last but not least Rena Wood.

CHAPTER 1 – EXCUSES

◆ ◆ ◆

'Pasta was not known in England'

◆ ◆ ◆

'Curry was a surname'

◆ ◆ ◆

'A takeaway was a mathematical problem'

Near Miss

Back in the mid-1980s my parents moved to a town in Greater Manchester called Hyde and soon after moving in decided to register with a local surgery. So off they went to the nearest surgery to complete the appropriate paperwork. They managed to speak to the receptionist who informed them the surgery only had one doctor who was extremely popular so unfortunately would not be able to take any new patients. Perhaps they could try again in a few months. Reluctantly, they had to sign on at the local health centre instead. "That's a poor excuse," said my mum, "No one's that popular! He just can't be bothered!" Anyway as time went on vacancies did start to appear at the popular doctors surgery, (nobody new why), but my parents decided it was too much trouble to change so they stayed with the local health centre. It was probably the best decision they ever made as that very popular doctor was none other than Harold Shipman who infamously became known as doctor death! This was one excuse for which I am eternally grateful.
*On 31 January 2000, Shipman was found guilty of the murder of fifteen patients under his care. A two-year-long investigation of all deaths certified by Shipman examined Shipman's crimes. The inquiry identified 218 victims and estimated is total victim count at 250, about 80 percent of whom were elderly women.

Graham Shaw

Who would be a rat?

Back in 2007, the company I worked for won a contract to refurbish/refit two gunships for small Pacific Island country. The terms of the contract stated that we would be paid in stage payments. The first tranche was one million pounds to be paid once we had taken over the first ship. This was duly invoiced, as requested by the Project Manager (PM). After six weeks payment had not been received and worries started to set in at head office. The PM was requested to chase up with the relevant government department. After a couple of days we received the following message. "We have not yet taken over the ship as it is infested with rats" Once this was resolved work and payments went ahead. When work was due to start on the second ship the first invoice was issued via the PM. After a couple of weeks I contacted the PM to confirm all was in order with the invoice and when we could expect payment. The reply I received back this time was: "Good news no rats aboard the second ship.... THE SNAKES HAVE EATEN THEM"

Bob Smith

Anyone for venison?

When I was working in the office we had ours reps coming in every few weeks to report and have a meeting with the other reps and the manager. There was one rep in particular that was always late and had so many excuses that nobody believed a word he said, so on this day the manager was getting quite angry as he was really very late. He strolled in as always and said "Sorry I'm late but on the way here I ran over a deer." "Really," said our Manager somewhat sceptically. "Yes, really I have, come and see in the boot of my car. Low and behold there was a deer in the boot with blood all over the reps blanket etc. The manager was shocked that for once the rep was telling the truth but said you should have reported it. "I have done" he said, "I have told you!" My manager was lost for words.

Rena Wood

Up north?

Further to the previous story. My manager was actually a bit of a hypocrite as he himself was renowned for his own excuses. He often said he was late or going to be late due to needing to go to site meetings!

We all knew of his excuses and in fact one of the young lads even kept a book of every time he mentioned another excuse in case he used it again and again.

On this particular day he said he was going 'up north' to meet someone on site. This immediately set the tongues wagging as he very rarely went to site and the few he did go to were in the south and, certainly not 'up north!'

It eventually came to light he had been having an affair with a girl up north and on this occasion his car number plate was caught speeding. Not a problem, it happens to most of us at some time or other. His big mistake however, was thinking the company would pay his fine. It was the investigation into this claim for expenses that eventually led to his downfall.

Rena Wood

Jungle Golf

I started golf in Freetown, Sierra Leone on a lovely course, rising from the blue sea up into the hills. The views were spectacular. Of course, there were different hazards in the tropics from those we are accustomed to in northern climes. The golf club used to run a monthly 'if only' competition for the best 'if only' excuse. Well, there were a few that I experienced. How about: If only that monkey had not come down from the tree and pinched my ball…… If only that venomous snake hadn't approached me just as I was about to play my shot…. If it hadn't been for the tropical storm that broke out half way through my round…. My caddie wasn't on form today. He should have found the ball that I sprayed into the woods on my left… I didn't like the look of that scorpion eyeing me as I played my bunker shot… It's too hot to play golf today…

Hugh Ball

Balls or Why I didn't win the Open'!

My company, Sierra Leone Brewery, sponsored the Sierra Leone Open Golf Championships. It was my job as Marketing Manager to organise the sponsorship activities. I decided amongst other things that we should provide balls for the competitors. Heineken, the technical partner in the brewery (my company, Unilever, was the commercial partner), had a business gifts catalogue in Amsterdam which included golf balls with the Heineken logo on them. I duly ordered 3 gross of them in good time to be handed out to competitors. Nice gesture I thought. I was more than a bit dismayed, therefore, when walking through the golf club car park behind two competitors, to hear the following conversion: "Do you know what balls they've given us for the Open this year?" "No, what are they?" "Bloody Wilson" was the response. Having just started the game myself, I was totally unaware as to how important the make of ball could be to serious golfers. This was the era when the ball of choice to anyone who, with pretensions to play the game properly, was the Dunlop 65i, a ball that came resplendently enclosed in a smart black paper wrapper. How times have changed! I have to confess that I have been put off Wilson balls and indeed Wilson equipment ever since!

Hugh Ball

Limbering up for the new job.....

Many years ago, I used a recruitment agency to hire a sales coordinator. After first and second interviews of those put forward by the agency, I offered the job to a lady who I considered very suitable and who I felt would bring new skills and experiences and fit in well with the rest of the team. I'll call her Jean (not her real name). In the offer of employment, I stated to Jean she should arrive on her first day at 10am. This would allow me to attend to the inevitable first-thing issues and be able to induct her thoroughly during her first day, free of distractions. Before Jean's start date, the rest of the team had been briefed, so when 10am came and Jean hadn't arrived, there were a few quizzical looks directed around the office, with people looking at the wall clock in an animated way, or pointing to their wristwatches, to make the point. When it got to 10:30, I called our recruitment agency and spoke to my regular contact, Grace, who had led the recruitment of Jean. Grace said she would make a call and get straight back to me, which she did, telling me that Jean's home phone wasn't answered (before the days of mobile phones) and that she would keep trying until she got an answer and would report back to me.

I caught-up with Grace later in the day and she had still been unable to contact Jean but said she would keep trying. Two days later, Grace called me and said she had managed to speak to Jean's Husband and had just come off of the phone to him. She relayed the conversation, where she had introduced herself and the situation to the Husband and asked why Jean hadn't shown up for her new job. The Husband replied: 'Oh, haven't you heard, she had a bad accident?' 'Oh, that's terrible. How is she now?' asked Grace. 'She is in hospital with her injuries. Both her legs and both arms are broken.' Grace was mortified: "How awful. What hospital and ward is she in. I must send her a card and flowers?' At this point, Grace told me that the Husband hesitated and couldn't recall the name of the hospital, then gave Grace the name, but couldn't remember the ward. Grace told me that, on the one hand, something didn't appear right to her, yet on the other hand, who would say such an awful thing if it weren't true? Grace said she would endeavour to find out the full story.

About 6-weeks past and we had heard nothing. In fact, we had hired someone else by the time. Grace phoned me one morning: "Do you recall Jean, the one who didn't show up for her first day with you?' How could I forget: 'Of course? Have you found out anything?' 'Yes I have. You know that Smith & Jones (not the real name) are one of our larger clients?' 'Yes, I remember you telling me.' 'Well, I was asked to visit them to help with recruiting a new person and when I walked through the sales office, who should I see there?' 'No, it surely wasn't Jean, was it?' 'Yes, I didn't notice her at first, as her back was to me as she was walking to her desk and when she turned to sit down, I clocked her straight-away. There was nothing wrong with her walking and both arms seemed to be working fine.' 'Did you say anything to her?' 'I wasn't there to see her, but I didn't need to say anything. She turned crimson red as soon as she realised it was me.'

Tim Franklin

California breeze…..

Back in 1979 I went on my first business to trip to the USA and was attending a conference at the Hotel del Coronado in San Diego, California. This is a very famous and prestigious hotel, having been the setting for Some Like It Hot and many other films and TV dramas. I settled into my huge poolside room, finding it hard to take in how big and how different everything was in the USA. My first cup of coffee was bucket-sized and being asked how I would like my breakfast eggs cooked – easy, over easy, well done, sunny side up – I'd never come across that before. To be told "Have a nice day or missing you already" were alien terms to me. Anyway, over the first day of my stay, several colleagues from the USA started to arrive. I knew one or two of them and I noticed that my colleagues had brought their wives with them. Not something we'd be allowed to do back in the UK (or Great Britain as we proudly called it in those days).

One of the colleagues I knew offered for him and his wife to take me out to a restaurant one evening and we arranged that I would meet them at the entrance to the hotel. At the given time, I stood under the entrance canopy of the hotel. Outside, it was a lovely Californian early evening, sunny and with a warm breeze. I recognised my colleague as he pulled-up in his car, with his wife in the passenger seat. He stepped out to greet me and his wife got out too, to allow me to climb into the rear seat of the two-door car. As I started to walk forward and down the steps towards them, I felt the breeze whip-up and became acutely aware of feeling the breeze where I normally would not – around my nether region! I immediately looked down and saw that my flies were gapping. All I could think was to make an excuse, to be able to retire to a safe place, where I could adjust my attire: "I've forgotten something,' I shouted and darted back into the hotel. Fortunately, there was a small shop just inside the lobby entrance and after finding a corner where I zipped my flies up, I went into the shop, grabbed and paid for a packet of cigars. Back outside, barely a minute later, I held up the cigars and announced: 'Sorry, I forgot to buy these earlier.' Did they see through my excuse? I'll never know.

Tim Franklin

January 1991, late getting home

I was only a couple of days late. We had to dodge a war... We had submitted a large tender near the end of 1990 to a large United Arab Emirates customer for some clever kit manufactured by the company I worked for at the time. It was an important order for us so instructions came down from on high to win the contract whatever the obstacles may be. Coincidentally, Saddam Hussein had decided to invade Kuwait a few months earlier and the international community were working hard to avoid a military scuffle in the Gulf. Hopefully.

We were called out for negotiations in early January 1991 whilst the UN and various other dignitaries were trying to negotiate with Saddam to vacate Kuwait. The invasion took place in August 1990 so it all seemed to be a fairly slow burning affair and anyway, Abu Dhabi was over 500 miles from Kuwait. No worries, let's go. It'll only take a few days. We'll be home in no time. So three of us jumped on a BA flight and checked in to the Meridian Hotel. A small, modest place to stay? Err... Not! There were only 14 restaurants to choose from. Negotiations proved to be tricky with the potential customers' procurement representative who was, in my memory, no more than 4ft 6in tall. He was feisty to say the least. My Arabic was not up to much but his tone, arm waving and the looks on the faces of his staff and our local representative were enough to figure out that he needed an anger management course (or three). We had largely parked in our minds UN Resolution 678 passed on 29 November 1990 requiring Saddam to exit Kuwait before 15 January 1991 or face military consequences. Our friendly customer possibly had not. He kept us there as we headed towards the deadline presuming that geo-political angle would exert pressure on us to meet his price requirement. Walk out with no order or drop the price. You choose gentlemen. At the appointed UN deadline time on 15 January, the alarm on my watch went off. I had set it to local time taking in to account the time difference from the UN resolution of midnight US Eastern Standard time. We were still there.

There were a total of five guests in the huge Meridien hotel. Getting a table in any of the 14 restaurants was not a problem. There were next to no cars on the roads. It was to say the least, weird. We had a meeting planned with Mr Excitable later that morning. We had stayed passed the deadline so we thought we had shown that we were not for bending so far on price and hopefully this would be the last meeting, we would agree a contract and then we could get on the BA flight leaving late that evening. It was the last scheduled flight in a somewhat disrupted timetable so we made reservations. No option really.

Good news; the meeting went to plan and we agreed a deal. Phew! We're heading home. Bad news; Abu Dhabi airport was like a zoo when we got there with people scrambling to get out before whatever was to come now that the UN deadline had passed. Also the plane was now going to Muscat in Oman to pick up there so the journey time would be extended by a couple of hours. Not quite there yet.

Dressed in full business garb, carrying brief cases and trying to look calm, the three of us made it on to the flight. Business class thank you very much. I sat next to the UK Ambassador's wife who was leaving her husband behind. She was apprehensive to say the least and somewhat teary eyed. That was not enough to distract me from falling asleep as soon as the wheels left the ground. No booze, no food, I was in need of a proper kip after a week of high drama. The adrenaline had stopped pumping. Out like a light. So much so, I later discovered that I had slept through the landing and take-off in Muscat. That's a first. The next thing I remember is being woken up by light coming through the plane windows and people moving about. The crew have started the pre-landing routine, breakfast is imminent. Fantastic news, we can only be an hour or so from Heathrow. Result. The next thing I notice through the curtain concealing the galley is the (male) steward crying. Perhaps the coffee machine had broken? Then the calm sophisticated voice of a BA Captain takes to the P.A. and we get the usual "hopefully you managed to get some sleep blah, blah, blah." All well and good but can Mr Blubby wipe away the tears and serve my much needed breakfast please.

Sitting to my left was one of my colleagues Brian. He opened the day with "the suns on the wrong side of the plane". Bloody engineers I thought. The most important issue in the world is my rumbling stomach and he's implying that the sun has magically shifted from its traditional position. He justified his statement with a theory that we should be travelling crudely north and therefore the morning sunrise should be to our right in the east. It was on the other side which meant we were travelling south. Holding pattern was my immediate reaction. Heathrow is always busy early morning. Our friendly Captain breaks out of standard mode on the P.A. to make an important announcement. Whilst we were somewhere over Riyadh last night, Saudi airspace was instantaneously closed to all commercial aircraft. George Bush (Snr.) and his mates had pushed the button. The armed assault on Saddam's troops in Kuwait had started.

Suddenly I had a different feeling in my stomach and I realised that Mr Blubby may need some sympathy rather than a rollicking for delaying my breakfast. The Captain went on, calmly, to explain that we had been instructed to "turn left" and land in Jeddah on the west coast of Saudi Arabia. The crew had quickly concluded that was not a great plan as we could be stuck there for a long time with the national no fly zone in place so Jeddah ATC were happy to wave to us as we flew over their heads towards Africa. Not enough fuel to skirt Libya and Algeria to get home (even with ATC clearance if that was even feasible) so Addis Ababa was the next logical airport with a runway long enough to land us on. Ethiopia. Hmmm. We took option 3. "If you take a look out of the window you will get a great view of the Rift Valley on our way down to Nairobi" said the Captain. "Don't worry, BA are committed to your safety and we'll look after you when we get there". He didn't mention anything about the sun having moved from its traditional position at the centre of our solar system so Brian's observation about us heading south had been satisfactorily explained and we were out of a war zone. Good news indeed. Now the Ambassador's wife immediately to my right didn't see it quite that way and full waterworks were in flow. I can't remember what I said to comfort her but I probably was not as well polished at these types of things as an experienced BA Captain. I'll leave it there.

Not too much conversation flowed after that but breakfast finally arrived (with coffee) garnished with a great view of the Rift Valley and we then landed in Kenya. So did two other BA planes that were en-route to Heathrow from India and Pakistan and in Saudi airspace just at the wrong time. We had us a convoy and something like 500 bodies arriving without any notice, an interesting challenge for the local BA rep. We soon learnt that the A/C system on a plane is powered by the main engines and when you sit on the tarmac in a big aluminium tube for a few hours (whilst BA did some hustling) in the hot Africa sunshine it can get a bit toasty. We also learnt that a visa was required to enter Kenya at that time so the local BA rep had been hard at work finding us hotel rooms and a deal to get through immigration. We eventually decanted from the plane and surrendered our passports to Kenyan immigration. I did wonder if we would ever see them again. There must be a market for a broad selection of 500 British Passports in Kenya surely? BA said it would all be OK so why worry. A bus ride later we arrived at the Hilton in the city. Sure enough BA had found us a room each and a welcome letter assured us that we were in good hands, they would keep us informed of developments, pay for meals (and non-alcoholic drinks) as long as we were there. Our luggage would follow ASAP. The hotel phone system was somewhat hit and miss (no mobiles then of course) so we managed to get a call through eventually to the office to tell them what was happening and contact families in case we couldn't.

Now, we were in a hotel dressed in business suits, nothing to change in to, hot and sweaty and no clue as to when we would be leaving. We did know that the BA crew had to rest for a significant period of time before they could fly again so what to do? Yes you've guessed it, head for the loungers by the pool and order some beers on BA. We switched to holiday mode. Our luggage did arrive and having established for certain that the BA crew were having a good nap, we changed into civvies and decided to take a wander round Nairobi. We knew that our company had a local representative there but we couldn't recall the name or address. If we could find the office by trial and error, we could perhaps use a better phone connection and make some calls. A great plan.

I had only previously heard about leprosy when reading the bible. I think I had concluded at school age that it was mythical. Believe me, it's not. There were plenty of roadside beggars taking a strong interest in these three strangers standing out from the rest of the Nairobi street people. There's nothing like a personal close-up view of some of the harsh realities of life to set some context for your own. Our walking tour of

Nairobi consequently didn't last too long especially when we remembered that the welcome letter said not to leave the hotel otherwise we might miss our ride home. Leg it.

Later that day, we were loaded back on to a bus and taken to the airport having been told that BA were not totally sure when we could depart but it was best to be there loitering with intent rather than sitting by the Hilton pool drinking beer or wandering around Nairobi. We dropped our bags, miraculously reclaimed our passports on the way through and then found a pew airside waiting for news. We've all done it but, in this instance, there was no set departure time and no departure board to hopefully stare at. The plastic chairs were about as uncomfortable as is imaginable so the less time the better in a hot terminal building please. We saw the crew mosey through the building (as they do) and board the plane which had to be a good sign. None of them were crying. Not long now. We didn't know too much about the goings on in Kuwait as live information was scarce but it appeared that some hell was raining down on the resident Iraqi army courtesy of the international coalition. The elite Iraqi Republican Guard were on the scene and had Iraq's latest tech so anything could happen. We didn't envisage Kenya being a target and it was definitely better than being in the UAE. Much time passed in the fairly dead terminal and our attempts to gain any useful information from the airport staff we could doorstep proved to be fruitless. The natives were becoming restless.

We eventually were approached asking for one representative to be appointed to be taken for a meeting with someone from BA. A bit of a strange arrangement we thought but we had Hobson's choice so we'll take it. Earlier, my travelling colleague Brian (the Engineer) had been the focus of attention noticing that the position of the sun needed an explanation. Now my other colleague (and boss) Stuart, 'volunteered' to be the passengers' representative. When I tell you that he was the Conservative candidate at the 1979 General Election for Chesterfield you will realise that he was not the shy and retiring type. Volunteered is the wrong adjective. 'Thrust himself forward' fits the bill better. Speculation was rife as to what news he would return with. If it was good news, surely someone would have come to hold forth to a happy crowd? My assumption was that news of the other variety was coming and someone from BA had worked out that having one person in front of them was better than a baying mob. Sometime later Stuart reappeared, and he had actually met our BA captain. He found a high vantage point to make like a politician with a crowd who need to be addressed. This is a movie scene now. An airport drama! What was the message to be? I forget the full explanation but, in a nutshell, the logistics of getting all the ducks in a row to enable the plane to depart had taken too long. Any air crew's working hours are strictly governed for safety reasons and the clock starts when they arrive at the airport. When adding the length of the flight to the delay we had already experienced, our crew was timed out. They can't take to the air and they were obliged mosey on back to their hotel for a kip (having not done very much). Nobody knew when the air travel ducks would be herded back into a neat row so we were in limbo. To add to the pain, we had to stay at the airport on 'hot standby' so no comfy hotel for us. It was certainly hot and we were every bit stood by.

More of those plastic seats and very little chance of any sustenance was the order of the day. Not great. So, what to do? No way of passing the time with an internet connection back then and we were captive in the terminal airside which was effectively closed. The best we could muster was a successful breaking and entering crime into the 1st class lounge which was empty on account of there being no planes scheduled to depart. The chairs and settees were infinitely more comfortable than the cheap garden furniture outside. We raided the fridges for drinks and devoured the stock of pretzels and assorted nibbles, all a relative luxury and no more than we deserved. We also had the benefit of a TV to catch up on the news from Kuwait. Unfortunately, the coverage was by the US network CNN which was christened 'Cockle Noodle News'. They showed a reporter pulling on a gas mask and diving under a table in fear of a gas attack. Comforting stuff. I'm not sure where he was but it may well have been a studio in California (where they filmed the moon landings obviously). Awful TV. Turn it over quickly and find some Tom and Jerry or the like. Proper violence. I did not have much idea of what day it was let alone the time of day but we made it on to the plane some hours later when the crew were suitably rested, the plane had enough fuel and ATC clearance all along the route. Even our luggage made it.

No dramas to report from this point onwards. Experience over. Credit must go to BA who did an exceptional job in the circumstances and we were thankful that we had not taken the Ryanair option (or whatever the equivalent was in 1991). As history now tells us, the 'war' turned in to a bit of a turkey shoot but Saddam managed to launch a few Scud missiles in the direction of Saudi Arabia and Israel and wrecked Kuwait. The Republican Guard was not so elite, the coalition (from 35 countries) had bigger sticks and Saddam got his backside tanned. As excuses go, 'we had to dodge a war' sounds a bit far-fetched but thanks to CNN's global reach its credibility stood up. We had met an ambassador's wife, been to three different countries (having planned to visit only one), witnessed a side of human existence that must be seen to be believed, starred in a disaster movie (of sorts), lorded it up in a first class lounge and saved the planet from a serious problem involving our sun. Oh and secured the all-important equipment order that made the adventure worthwhile. I think.

Richard Stone

CHAPTER 2 - GROWING UP

◆ ◆ ◆

'Pizza was something to do with a leaning tower'

◆ ◆ ◆

'All crisps were plain'   The only choice we had was whether to add the salt from the little blue bag

◆ ◆ ◆

'A Chinese Chippy was a foreign carpenter'

◆ ◆ ◆

'Sunday's was always a roast dinner with the family'

MR MEL LOCKETT

Youthful memories of childhood times in the Potteries

I spent a few years as a youngster in grim, grimy Burslem, one of the five towns which make up Stoke on Trent or the Potteries. Stoke itself, surprisingly, does not exist as a town. So looking for it proves tricky for visitors! We lived in one of the poorest parts of Burslem, with most of the back to back houses having no railings or fences because all the iron had been taken for the war effort. Several houses in our street were condemned properties, ours only allowed living downstairs. Polio was a big scare with seven cases in our short block.

The only useable toilet was of course outside at the end of our brick back yard. In winter it was freezing cold and often you had to break the loo ice before you could go! Toilet paper didn't exist, but the upside was that the torn strips of newspaper made great reading, especially when bits of the Beano were on offer! You had also to time your visits, having to make sure you did not coincide with the firing of the bottle shaped pottery kilns behind our house. If you got it wrong, you got covered with black sooty particles all over you!

Up the street was a pub which had a peculiar beer delivery habit. Young boys like me were sent with a can like jar which was filled with beer to deliver home.

The local school was a gem. It was surrounded on three sides by closed factories and on the fourth by a really exciting bomb site. Dining arrangement were a bit ad hoc as the school had no dining room, so lunchtime dinners came in large metal boxes delivered to a communal hall for three schools. The noise was total. Any spare spuds or veg were launched on your dessert spoon towards rival school kids. If you were caught out, punishment was instant and painful. I still recall the burning pain on my fingers from the cane. Crafty attempts to lower your hand at the very last moment of the bamboo strike, usually led to further pain.

One thing which also sticks in the memory is the strange language of the area. First second and third were foggy, seggy, peggy, yennie, yennie, yennie, I never did understand it other than it had something to do with having something! Highlight of the month were the gifts from visiting Canadian soldiers, who gave out raisins and chocolate powder to us. This was a vast improvement on the minuscule offerings from the tyrannical old lady Maggie who ran the sweet shop. She extracted large units of ration book points in return for a minimal number of sweets, which never included my favourite rhubarb and custard. My first banana was an interesting eating experience as I did not know you had to peel it first!

My only claim to fame in these times was that football legend, Sir Stanley Mathews had a brother, who cut my hair, I warmly remember an early Christmas present, which my Dad spent all night making. He painted a spare door with a whole street map of our area and added a Dinky car to play on it. It was the best present I ever had being made with so much love.

Mike Williams

My childhood memories of the nineteen fifties and sixties.

When I was growing up our Dinner time was at a regular time. Every Sunday it was a roast at 1.00 pm, simple as that!

Eating out was not heard of, we only had a take away on special occasions. We only received a present on birthdays and at Christmas. None of this Halloween, Easter and congratulations you have a pulse day.

Fast food was fish and chips and having a bottle of panda pop from the shop was a real treat.

You took your school clothes off as soon as you got home and put on your 'playing out' clothes, - children looked like children, we didn't pout, wear makeup or have anxiety.

There was no taking or picking you up in the car, you walked or rode your bike!

Our house phone had a cord attached, so there was no such thing as private conversations or mobile phones! Ours was out in the hall.

We didn't have Now TV, Sky, Netflix or Amazon Prime. We could watch three channels only. Channel 4 and 5 were exciting additions! We had to watch all of the adverts unless we switched to BBC.

We played Army, British Bull Dog, Kerby (Ed note. Popular in Scotland), Hide & Seek, knock or door run, Tag, Football, climbed trees, made mud pies, daisy chains, rose perfume never smelt brill and rode bikes.

Everyone could play ball! We used tops, jumpers or jackets for goalposts and even made a ball out of paper if we needed to.

A wheelie and bunny-hop on your bike was a standard skill and we used to put cards in the spokes so it sounded like a motorbike.

Staying in the house was a PUNISHMENT and the only thing we knew about "bored" was --- "You better find something to do, before I find it for you!"

We ate what mum made for our Dinner, or we ate nothing at all. If we rushed our Dinner we weren't allowed to go back out and if we didn't eat it, we weren't allowed back out either.

Bottled water was not a thing; we drank from the tap.

We had scraps, some we lost, some we won but we always had a go back.... Or we got another one when we got home.

We watched cartoons on the TV on Saturday mornings, and rode our bikes for hours and just simply ran around.

We weren't AFRAID OF ANYTHING. We played till dark... street lights were our alarm clock.

If someone had a fight, that's what it was and we were friends again a week later, if not SOONER.

We watched our MOUTHS around our elders because ALL of our aunts, uncles, grandpas, grandmas, AND our parents' best friends were all extensions of our PARENTS and you didn't want them telling your parents if you misbehaved, or they would give you something to cry about.

Everyone had respect.

I did my research by borrowing books from the public library. The Internet was non-existent and no Google!

We saw toys in adverts and had to wait until 'Santa' came before we expected. For me, these were the good days.

Roger Vaughan

The 6 year old brickie

We lived in Addiscombe, Croydon (not to be confused with the newer Addington), a pleasant older residential area. My Grandad who was a bricklayer with British Rail said he would rebuild the crumbling brick wall fronting our house. I loved my old Grandad and wanted to help. I was just six years old and I guess I became the youngest brickies mate that maybe today would be called a go-fer! The wall took a couple of days to build with me fetching bricks for Grandad while he laid them. These bricks were a reddish colour. Thinking back I'm not sure where they came from but they definitely were not British Rail blue! When finished the wall stood out compared to adjacent houses.

This would have been 1949 and in more recent years (2014ish), I drove back to Eastbourne from London 'the old way' via Brixton, Upper Norwood and Woodside to reminisce, before making my way home. Certainly the late Arthur Fenton, my grandad left his mark as the wall is still there. Colin Wood will remember the Black Horse Pub opposite our road which I happily drove the car up but which was now one way, well I was only going one way! Before I was forced to turn round just opposite my old house I was amazed to note our little red brick wall was still standing - perhaps I missed my true vocation?

Ray Fry

Bankruptcy pending

I was brought up in a Fish & Chip shop in Intake, Sheffield. My dad had a very good reputation for his food and had many customers who would travel past other chippies to get their Fish & Chips from him. I have lots of fond memories of my time in the 1940s and 50s. We were not rich by any means but having a Fish & Chip shop my parents did have a bit more spare cash than most families living around us. We had a car when owning a car was rare, and in 1951 we were first to have a TV in the area, albeit when we first got the TV we could only watch the test card as our signal came from Sutton Coalfield in the midlands as Yorkshire did not have a transmitter then. It was several months before we could actually watch programmes.

Chips were 2d and fish 4d and I remember the concern and lengthy discussion my mum and dad had when deciding to put his fish up to 4½d and the effect it might have on his customers. This would be around 1947 just after World War 2 with rationing being the order of the day, so times were difficult for a lot of people.

My parents taught me and my siblings the meaning of hard work insisting on certain tasks being carried out each week. One in particular was 'doing the spuds'. Each Wednesday night my brothers and I had to prepare five x 1cwt (one hundredweight) bags, of potatoes. This entailed shovelling raw potatoes, sometimes with mud still on them, into a 'rumbler' which removed the skin. They were then tipped into a tub of warm water. It had to be warm as during the winter months the outhouse where we did the spuds would be freezing.

My dad was a stickler for ensuring there was not a blemish on his potatoes, so we had to handle each spud and where necessary remove the 'eyes' or remaining skin before throwing them into a 'bosh' of clean water, ready for 'chipping' when needed.

The whole process was repeated on Saturday morning but this time only 3 or 4 cwt.

On Friday night's my pals and I would play cards, usually 'three card or seven card brag', before sitting down and watching 'The Army Game' on a small black and white TV. We would be 15 or so. My younger brother would be 11 or 12 years old and always wanted to join us. He inevitably lost at cards and he will tell you the post cards conversation then went something like this.

Me. "That's 3/6d you owe me".
Brother. "I don't have 3/6d".
Me. "You do my spuds in the morning and I will let you off".
Brother. "OK".

So much for me and the hard work ethic my parents taught us! Funny, but it was my brother who was the one to follow my parents into the business.

My clearest memory however was as a 15 year old being made to serve in the shop. My first occasion, dressed in my oversized white coat, was one Tuesday evening. Tuesday was always a quiet night. One of the first customers was a lad I recognised but not one of my close friends. He asked for Fish & Chips. I served him and was just wrapping them up in old newspaper lined with greaseproof paper, when my dad came through from what we called the fish-place, (where he filleted and prepped his fish). He watched me take the one shilling proffered, give the lad 3d change (Fish was by then 6d and chips 3d) and off went the satisfied customer.

There I am, chest stuck out and quite pleased with myself having served my first customer. However, my world was about to crumble. The next thing I hear is my dad's booming voice saying, in his strong South Yorkshire accent, "Tha'll bloody bankrupt us, tha's gi'n him a bobs' worth of chips theer lad".

I then got a lesson in portion control!

Mel Lockett

Out & about - playtime

There were a number of roads linking the Lower Addiscombe Road with the parallel Bingham Road and all the back gardens were in turn linked by back alleyways, a brilliant playground for us kids, knock down ginger, cowboys and Indians, hide & seek and many variations from these themes. So through the fifties from around 7 - 10 years old these were our days of fun. I was nearly caught on a couple of occasions risking 'knock down ginger,' *(Ed note. Another version of 'knock or door run')* which basically entailed knocking on a victims' door and running off before the door was opened, a prank that was in fact made illegal as long ago as the mid-19th century. The term "knock down ginger" apparently derives from part of a children's' rhyme which went:

Ginger, Ginger broke a winda

Hit the winda' – crack!

The baker came out to give 'im a clout

And landed on his back.

The game is played in one form or another under various names, all over the world. I suppose the most popular game however was cowboys and Indians - we all had Cowboy hats, belts, holsters, plastic guns, bows and arrows etc., and lacking local prairies we played it though the back alleyways and adjacent roads (I wish I still had that kind of energy!). One of the gangs' parents were a bit better off than most of us who gave Roger a fully chrome plated replica of a Colt 45 which made a resounding noise when fired with caps and which cost £2.7s.6d (£2.37p) which was a lot of money in those days and was coveted by all of us. Roger occasionally let us hold it but never out of his sight!

Ray Fry

Cotton Bobbin Tank

Growing up in the 1950s we learned to create our own entertainment and toys. Money was scarce so we had to use what we could lay our hands on. One of the many things we made was what we called Cotton Bobbin Tanks. You scrounged around your mums sewing basket or box, looking for almost empty wooden cotton reels. You unravelled and discarded the remaining cotton, which was not needed for the tank, whilst always being wary of a clip around the ear-hole from mum, if caught. You would then cut notches in the rims of the reel to give it some grip. Then with the aid of a matchstick, a longer piece of wood or a pencil, an elastic band and a piece of wax or candle you assembled your tank and tested it. As kids we would then meet up and have races to see whose tank could go fastest or farthest. I wonder if this practical, hands-on activity is what led us to be a nation of engineers?

The image is of one I made recently to test my memory, and YES, it worked.

Ray Fry

I wet myself.

Growing up back in the 1950s I seemed to have a lot of freedom to play out. My parents owned a fish & chip shop so tended to be working a lot of the time especially on Saturdays with both lunch and evening openings. One particular memory is walking from our shop with my pal Andy and my elder brother Tony, down Jaunty Lane and across what we called the 'long fields' (now all houses) to the Old Harrow pub (now an Indian restaurant), across more fields, passed a couple of farms owned by the Fiddler brothers and eventually to the little village of Ridgeway and then down the hill into Ford. I would be about nine or ten at the time, still in short trousers, and my brother four years older.

Ford is a beautiful village some three and a half miles from home and which, at the time had the attraction of a mill dam and a waterwheel, unfortunately no longer there. We followed the little stream below the dam for about a quarter of a mile, just playing and generally enjoying ourselves on a warm sunny summer's day. I saw a small dam wall crossing the stream in the middle of which was a very large stone. I ventured to the middle of the wall and bent down to push the stone over the dam wall. However, I knew little about physics and instead of the stone tumbling over the dam I fell backwards into the dam. As a ten year old it appeared to be very deep but in reality was about two feet of water. I was absolutely soaked to the skin.

My now newly responsible brother took charge and decided we should go home. He must have had some sympathy for me; most unusual I have to say; and decided we should catch the bus home, a single decker if I remember correctly. It was fortunate that he had a few pence in his pocket for the fare. My clothes still wet and dripping, and the bus conductor would not let me sit down making me stand all the way home.

MR MEL LOCKETT

Mel Lockett

Coincidence or what?

Further to the 'I wet myself' story, on a visit back to Sheffield in 2021, my eldest son asked me where I would like to go. I told him I would like to re-visit the village of Ford and have a pint in the Bridge Inn, something I could not do in 1950. We arranged to go in the afternoon. Earlier that same day I went to visit George the father of my son-in-law, a spritely ninety four year old, at his home.

Imagine my surprise then when I entered his lounge and saw a large painting of The Bridge Inn, hanging above his fireplace.

It turned out that the Bridge was the favourite hostelry of George and his wife Muriel, often visiting twice a week for a lunch. Needless to say George came with us and we both enjoyed a lovely pint and shared our memories of the past.

Mel Lockett

Nose Dive!

WARNING – This story contains humour and slang which may offend Wokes and others of a sensitive disposition. It may also contain nuts, particularly if referencing the author...

Being into my mid 20's I had achieve some of the proportions of a well formed athlete, sufficient to appeal to young women when adorned in no more than a pair of budgie smugglers. Thus it was when on a trip to Leatherhead swimming pool with my dear friends Mike and Shawen I spied a couple of girlies in the pool giving me 'the look'! Having only recently learned to do a backward dive, now was probably not the right time to use it to impress, but such thoughts would have to assume a certain level of maturity not present in a young 'stag'. Even if the time hadn't been wrong, the timing of my dive and everything that followed definitely was!

Leatherhead swimming pool, for those who may have visited in the early 80's sported a decent size swimming area and a dedicated diving pool kitted out with a 1 and 3 meter spring board alongside a massive 5 meter concrete platform. I'm not sure that such structures still exist in public places after health and safety having wreaked havoc on most forms of fun, but even if it did, then the litigation culture would have sealed the fate of those willing to offer it. Fortunately dear reader, my story is set in the 80's when life was for living, and risk for the taking. It requires courage to jump off a 5 meter board, and pure madness to dive off it, but fortunately I had neither the courage or stupidity to do either. But the 3 meter board was a different story...

At this point I need to confess. Up until then I had only ever dived off backwards from a 1 meter board, and when I say dived off backward, what I really mean is that I stood with my back facing out into the pool and simply 'piked' into the dive. But today was going to be different, purely on account of two attractive and attentive girls watching me from the side of the main pool and luring me to my fate! I started by scaling the 3 meter board and standing adonis like with my back to the pool. After taking my time and bouncing a few times to draw as much attention as possible it was clear that my tactics were having the desired effect, and after just one warm up dive I had secured the undivided attention of those that mattered. It was now time to perform with a spectacular dive that would give me the opportunity, once completed, to slip into the main pool alongside those two beauties and claim my reward.

Back up the board I went, but this time I had more purpose, mindful that the prize which awaited me was going to be easier to win the better I did. I strolled nonchalantly to the end of the board, turned slowly and stood there magnificently. A bounce or two would signal the start of the main event but not before I had looked down over my left shoulder to make sure my little babes were giving me the attention I craved. Sure enough, there they were, heads wresting on arms that hung over the poolside, giggling together and meeting me eye to eye. Job done! And so it began, two bounces, each one bigger than the other, followed by a third and final compression of the board flexing it downwards with such force that the stored energy would hurl a full size man high into the air over the water where fate, or skill, would determine the outcome.

Just one problem... in all the excitement I had forgotten a vital move... As anticipated my body was indeed launched high enough to perform the perfect pike, but I had failed to propel myself outward and away from the board. I was now in the head down, feet down position watching my toes glide slowly past the end of a returning board that was coming up to meet me head to head! Too late, the board smashed into my face, straightening me up like a bean pole and dropped me feet first into the pool. Down, down I went. A fog of grogginess surrounded me as I realised that this had gone rather badly! But hey, I was young, determined and bold and in those few seconds of composition I gathered myself and decided that I would simply surface, smile and behave as if nothing was wrong. And so it was. From the bottom of the pool, I looked up at the shimmering light high above and swam to break cover ready to do it all again.

But what was this? No sooner had I appeared from the depths and struck out for the side when my two lovely chicks started screaming. Odd I thought, particularly as the water around me was an unexpected shade of claret and an unprecedented level of activity was going on poolside. Seconds later I was being dragged out of the water by two life guards who placed my head backwards in an effort to staunch the flow of blood, and frog marched off to the first aid room. My final memory of that fateful evening was an ambulance ride to hospital and 6 stiches in my nose. Sadly the doctors could do nothing to save my hurt pride, or to heal my sadness that I would never get to chat to those beautiful girls!

PS. Had this happened today then things would have been very different. The pool would have been permanently closed, the owners sued, and I would have been awarded over 50 million quid for permanent brain damage affecting my cognitive skills and consequential loss of earnings as a major international golf pro! Oh yes, and naturally I would have gone on to marry both girlies, had loads of babies and lived happily ever after!

Adrian Beal

The 'Brum' of my youth

Birmingham is an amazing place, being wonderfully Irish, gloriously Jamaican and very proudly Brum. As a city, its culture divides the nation, a bit like Marmite; you either love it or hate it. What you can't do is ignore it. Maybe a short introduction to its vowel rich midlands accent will help the dissenters. There are a couple of essential verbs you need to know to be able to decipher the accent. 'Djow' and 'Loiyk' as in "Djow loiyk eet ere?" meaning "Do you like it here?" or "Djow theenk eets noyce?" meaning "Do you like the taste?" or "I loiyk eet," meaning "I Like it."

Now we are getting somewhere we can move on to essential pronunciation. Just add 'ING' to everything, such as singING, dancING and oiytING (eating). Numbers have their own unique sound, wun, taw, troy, fawer, and foive etc, and finally adjectives such as 'groyt' (great) and 'triffeek' (very good). It is an accent that is easy to get into but once there is very difficult to lose.

My first experience of Brum was moving from one flat to another opposite Small Heath Street, which ran from Coventry Road to Green Lane. When we arrived at our new location we were the only non-Brummies' there and when we left we were the only whites! First the Irish ran the buses then later on it was the Jamaicans. Both were equally cheerful and fun to be with.

My Dad went out of his way to ensure I had a chance of passing my 11 plus, the national examination at the age of eleven that decided your route in senior education. For three months he took me to the other side of Birmingham for 11+ coaching. Without that coaching I would have had no chance; being in a class of fifty in my inner city Primary School; of getting into Grammar School. I was awarded a place at King Edwards V1 Camp Hill Grammar School. Thanks Dad.

The school was located in the City centre sandwiched between major factories and the railroads. One of our main activities was swimming at the famous old Moseley Swimming Baths, a beautiful old building, which is still open today.

One added advantage was a local newsagents nearby which displayed the magazine 'Health & Efficiency' in which you could find photos of naked nubile young girls, one of the few magazines where young boys could get their first experience of girlish delights.

(Ed note. Ironically, I used to go swimming on Friday evenings at Glossop Road baths in Sheffield and on the way home used to look forward to passing a newsagents on Division Street with Health & Efficiency on show for a sneaky look at a nude woman).

I recall also the somewhat lethal playground game of 'Polly on the mop stick'! Two teams of boys took it in turns to try and collapse the others line of bent over bodies. It was eventually banned as too dangerous by 'elf n safety'. I loved it.
(Ed note. This game was played all over the UK under various names. In the North East it was called 'Montakitty' and in South Yorkshire 'Finger, thumb, rusty bum'. It is still played around the world where 'elf n safety' has not yet got a foothold).

The school, along with the sealed off girls school next door was moved to leafy Bourneville. There was a constant delicious smell of chocolate from the Cadbury's factory in the valley below. The outer circle bus route went past the school so everyone met on the buses. You soon got to know your favourite seat where your pals would be.

The bell skirt so popular with girls in the 1950s was especially exciting, voluminous skirts clipped in a huge circle by a solid plastic band. It made going upstairs an eye opener.

If you came from a posher outer suburb, you took the Midland Red Bus. If you lived out near the airport you would often see the Birmingham City players train as well as getting a rare sight of a tatty plane.

Yes the 'Land of Brum' had it all going then. There were famous factories like BSA, Singer Sewing machines, Fort Dunlop, Birds Custard, HP Sauce, Typhoo Tea, and the Lucas factory, as well as the car factories. Birmingham was the manufacturing centre of the world. In addition there was the wondrous jewellery quarter and let's not forget the Faggot and Pea shops. 'Brum is a great place with great memories.

Mike Williams

Two Little Boys

It was a glorious sunny day back in 1962, rare nowadays but commonplace back then. I was 9 and my friend and near neighbour Paul was a year or two older. We met up about 09.30 as normal and off we went to a grassy area at the foot of the Downs where many children of our age would meet. Some would get together and play in groups and some would go their own way to find amusement.

Unusual for Paul and I we chose to venture a bit further afield on this occasion. This being so long ago I can't be specific about the route we took but I would expect it to have been close to the following. Our first location would probably have been passing the second green at our beloved Willingdon, this only being about 150 yards from where the other kids were playing. We would have then turned left walking parallel to the third fairway, except in those days the tree line we walked in front of would have been about 40 yard from the fairway looking down a grass bank.

Half way along this stretch was a large oak tree which could probably be seen from the clubhouse, this tree was known by various names such as Old Oakey, the Pilot tree and no doubt a few others. This tree stood high on a bank and virtually always had a rope attached to one of the branches for those brave enough to swing on it, my time was yet to come. When added to the bank a fairly respectable height could be achieved at the furthest point out from the tree. It was quite common to see young lads lad's lose their grip midway through their swing and sail through the air before crashing back to earth, most of them survived with no major injuries,

From about the third green we would have followed a path a

short distance inside the woods. This would have taken us past a dew pond which lies about 20 yards from the sixth tee. Back in the day this dew pond would have been relatively clean and would probably have been a spot where we would have stopped and played for a while. The last time I walked this path the pond was now full of mud, fallen branches and rotting vegetation.

For the next stretch of our trek we would have followed the path which runs around the back of the twelfth green and then parallel to the path which takes us to the thirteenth tee. This path would then veer slightly away from the course to where it picks up the gully beside the fourteenth tee and eventually becomes the path adjacent to the boundary fence further down. A short distance below the fourteenth tee we would have turned left where we found ourselves in what would have been the garden of a once impressive residence. The house itself no longer stood, demolished I would assume prior to the building of the Ratton estate which at this time did not exist. In the garden was a large outdoor swimming pool lined with mosaic tiles but by now devoid of any water. There was also a well which was filled in with earth to within a few feet of the top. These two features would both be associated with rumours which were almost definitely fictitious. The gardens and the pool were said to be part of an old Roman villa, had this been true I'm sure they would have been preserved and exist to this day. Rumour had it that the well was filled in because a mother had thrown a baby into the well, more likely to have been filled in once the property was knocked down to prevent intruders, yours truly, from falling in (Health and Safety in 1962). We ventured to another area of the garden where we found what I would describe as an ornamental lily pond which unlike the pool did contain water. This looked too inviting to ignore and within minutes it was shoes and socks off and we went paddling amongst the lilies.

Our day of exploration was now about to come to an abrupt end. The peace and quiet of the lily pond was shattered by the scream of "There you are" coming from the lips of my eldest sister accompanied by her best friend Daphne. She informed us that we had now been missing for about 8 hours and a search party comprising family members, friends and even the police had been hunting for us for quite a while. The homeward trek now had to be endured with the occasional piggy back from my sister; after all this exploring is tough work. By all accounts once we were back home my father was not too pleased, understandably, but mum was just pleased we were home safely. As a parent I now fully appreciate the gravity of the ordeal I put my parents through and wouldn't wish it on any parent.

Alan Elms

Early school days

From our house to my first school Ashburton Primary was around 2 miles and we used to walk there and back whatever the weather often playing football in Ashburton Park on the way home. Note: A school run was something you did on sports day. We were allowed to play football, chase and rounder's in the playground but I seem to remember the favourite pastime in the early fifties was collecting cigarette cards, which came free in packets, (originally cigarette packets). The cards had images of everything you could think of, from film stars, footballers, cricketers, ships, aeroplanes, to flowers and trees etc. We used to exchange cards to try to make up a set or more likely play a game to win them from a friend. You flicked a card, in turn, against a wall and won one if you covered another. They were also collected in sets and often framed and may be quite valuable these days?

School dinners were obligatory where we formed a queue with a plate and utensils and were served with whatever slop was cooked on that day. We sat down at long tables and you were expected to clear your plate! Isn't that how they serve meals in prisons today? Overall though, these were good times although I do remember our arithmetic teacher, Ms Ferguson a small domineering woman who we all hated and were scared of. She wouldn't get a job these days.

Ray Fry

MR MEL LOCKETT

A Day off School

When I was twelve I was at school in Rochester. We were playing about in the school playground when I was asked by the Head master to follow him to his study. Three other boys were also asked to follow him. We did so with great trepidation wondering what misdemeanour we were about to be punished for. To our surprise the Head told us that a film company was making a film part of which was to be made in Rochester and the Producer needed four children of our age to take part in the film. Instead of the expected punishment we were asked if we would agree to be selected. We all readily agreed. We were told that we were needed the following day and we were to report to the Bull Hotel which was the Company's base for the duration. As time was short we were asked to obtain our parents' consent, duly given in all cases. Next morning we turned up at the Bull where we were told who would be in charge of us for the day.

This was something of a let-down. We were all hoping for a month off school. We were then told the film was called 'The Seekers'. The film was staged in 1820. It starred Jack Hawkins and Glynis Johns. During the film the two stars returned from New Zealand to their home in Rochester. They would arrive in a horse drawn cab and we were required to play the part of four children playing in the street as the cab arrived.

We were then told we would be provided with clothing appropriate to 1820. This was duly extracted from a large wicker trunk and allocated according to the size of the garment. To my dismay the first three suits were duly appropriated and the last garment was a girl's dress. It comprised a long powder blue dress with quantities of petticoats and a large broad brimmed hat. At that age I felt there was no way that I could wear it. One of the other boys suggested I should wear it because I had curly hair appropriate to the garment. Our chaperone said my hair was irrelevant as we would all be provided with long hair wigs. My attitude changed as I felt that none of us would be recognised. The idea of returning to school for Latin and maths certainly did not appeal! We were helped to put on the complex clothing and then off to be allocated our wigs and then to the make-up artists. We were told that as the cab arrived we would be playing a selection of games appropriate to the period so we were given tuition in "paper and scissors", bowling a hoop with a cane (me), and assembling a chair from lengths of cane and other period games.

We then moved to the first site for the filming where the road had been strewn with sand, road names and street lights had been covered with ivy and other disguises. We had a number of practice runs on site before the cameras moved in and the horse drawn cab made a number of trial arrivals. What no one could have anticipated was the arrival of the whole of our class (less 4) for a lesson in the music room which just happened to be in one of the buildings in the very street where we had been filming. Despite our clothes and wigs it took no more than a minute for the four of us to be recognised which caused great mirth all round. Fortunately the music master soon arrived and the class proceeded inside.

We and the film crew enjoyed a snack lunch after which we went to another part of Rochester (duly disguised) and spent the next hour or so practising and then running the sequence again in case the Producer was not happy with the original location and our efforts. We then returned to the Bull to have all make-up removed and our own clothing returned. Finally we received a visit from the Producer who thanked us for our endeavours and then gave instructions for us to be paid five shillings each for our efforts. As this was about two weeks pocket money we most impressed.

About 18 months later we heard that the film was about to be screened. I went with my parents to watch it at our local cinema. To my surprise it lasted about three hours. I was also surprised that there was a queue about two hundred yards long waiting to buy tickets. Fortunately there were seats left when we reached the front. Just as well because the Saturday night showing we went to was the last one before the film moved on. Next time I saw the film was several years later on television. The screen time had been cut to about one and a half hours. This virtually excluded all the appearance time of the four children in Rochester. If you blinked you would have missed us.

Malcolm Rolfe

Early life in East Yorkshire

I was born and bred in Yorkshire. Born in Hull in the late 1930s but most of my early life was in Great Hatfield which is near Hornsea on the east coast of Yorkshire and has the largest lake in Yorkshire called Hornsea Mere. I spent most of my time working on the local farms. I usually moved to another farm at the end of the harvesting season and went to the farmer currently paying the highest wages. As an example my hourly wage increased each year from one shilling and six pence, (£0.08) to one shilling and nine pence (£0.09) – for a 45 hour week - big stuff.

My mother died when I was nine years old and we moved in with my dad's sister - my Auntie Olive who was the mainstay of the chapel in the village and the local piano teacher. I'm afraid she failed dismally with me in both areas. I attended the local school in the village until I got to the Grammar school in Hull via the local 11+ examination. My days at the Grammar school were good. We played plenty of football and cricket. My dad and I played for the local teams in both sports until my dad packed up at the age of fifty.

I used to go into Hull for school at the Grammar school on the local trains until it was cut out during the 1950s. I had to catch a train which arrived at a station three stops from Paragon which was and still is the main station in Hull. To catch this particular train I had to persuade the teacher to let me leave bang on time and then I had to run like hell to catch the train I needed to get me to Goat Hatfield. I was very fit in those days.

My main jobs at the farms were spud picking or harvesting. If I wasn't doing these jobs I used to be kicked out in the field to knock a few weeds down. The work at spud picking was very straight forward but tiring. Harvesting was a much more complex job. These, of course, were the days before the combine harvester.

Our biggest piece of machinery was the wheat binder which was used to pick up the loose straw and put some binding string round each bundle and drop it for later collection. This is where the difficult part came in. My job was to work with the rest of the men to pick up the sheaves of whatever the crop was and build them into 'stooks', a group of 6 or 8 sheaves of grain stacked to dry vertically in a rectangular arrangement at harvest time. This job was really hard. It was always done in the heat of the summer so we usually had our shirts off which made for really bad sunburn.

The other problem was that each crop had a different method of pulling large quantities of skin from your body. Surprisingly the worst crop was barley which had long and very sharp straw attached to each head of the crop. There was no way to avoid these hazards apart from wearing a thick pullover. So it was a hard decision before we started each day. The other bad crop was wheat which was difficult because of the weight of each sheaf.

If I wasn't spud picking or harvesting my job would be milking which was the most pleasant job on the whole farm. My job would be to attach the mechanised milking pump to the cow and step back quickly in case it decided to have a fart which was a regular occurrence. The reward came at the end of the day when we had a drink of milk which had just gone through the cooling machine. It was absolutely delicious.

Another job I got regularly was in helping to shift the manure from the fold yard which led into the milking parlour. The manure had to be picked up with two tined forks. The cart we used was pulled by the local farm horse which believe it or not was called Dobbin. The man who controlled Dobbin had enormous skill. He would get the empty cart into the fold yard whilst standing on the cart and issuing commands to Dobbin. He almost never had to repeat himself.

My dad in the fifties and sixties used to be a building foreman for a builder in Hornsea. Naturally he attracted a lot of work in the village and always had some project in hand. My proudest moment came in this period. I had been working on the current farm all day but had arranged to leave about 4.00 pm to help my dad with some concreting. I was hard at it when I heard a tractor going past and looked up to the sound of men clapping. I stood up to find the men I had just been working with clapping me as they went past on the tractor and one man shouted out "Well done lad" A moment to remember!

I was brought up during World War 2 and one day during somebody mentioned that a German fighter plane had been shot down just outside the village. My mum allowed me to go and see it with some other boys. When we got there we found one policeman guarding it. There was no sign of the pilot so we guessed that he had already been picked up. There was a parachute on the floor which was completely covered in blood and the aircraft was almost completely destroyed. I can still see it.

Bill Prest

Born a Manxman

My Father was a shopkeeper; having been left the business aged 14. This was a grocers and dairy shop. Every weekend morning I would help deliver glass bottles of milk to the residents across the small ex capital of the Isle of Man, Castletown. Until I was 14 we even delivered milk on Christmas Day! My father was famous for his home-made ice-cream which he only made between the months of May and September. Freshly made every day we would have cars parked outside the shop with occupants eating 2 or 3 fresh cornets. These were not local residents but visitors who had just endured 4 hours across the Irish Sea from Liverpool that morning and who were returning the same day!

Most of you will not be aware that Policemen in the Isle of Man have winter and summer uniforms. That is, they wear white helmets in the summer months. Please don't ask me why. The local police station was but 10 minutes' walk away from our shop and during the summer we would always see the local bobby walking up the street and he knew us all.

If I did anything untoward my parents knew about it before I'd even got home. However, times were much quieter then and the bobby would have time to chat or drop into our shop. This is where the white helmet worked. He would purchase a handmade wafer of the ice-cream and it would be double wrapped in greaseproof paper. Why so, you may ask? Paid for he would gently place the package under his helmet and leave without delay. Up the street another 300 meters and around the corner, out of sight the package would be retrieved and enjoyed.

They were the days. I guess if he had been delayed after purchase any seepage would have at least been white against white. I am proud to say that on three occasions our ice-cream was dessert for Her Majesty the Queen when she came to lunch with Lord and Lady Gort who lived just round the corner.

John Court

Wet cycling

As a Manxman growing up on an Island surrounded by the Irish Sea you won't be surprised to learn that school holidays were mostly spent close to or in salty water. Days on the rocks, fishing or just messing about were just part of our early years. No issue about safety in those days, out in the morning, home when hungry whether lunch time or later. Close to home (harbour and rocks/beach a ten minute walk) or further afield on bikes not designed for off road. Aged 12, my mate and I had been out all day and cycling like mad things we had made it back to Castletown Harbour. A harbour overlooked by the magnificent Castle Rushen, a superbly preserved medieval castle open to the public. We were only five minutes from home but still with boundless energy and time to spare we were riding and skidding along the harbour arms and having a great time until said mate hit the harbour edge with his front wheel at speed.

Now we all know what happens when your front bike wheel suddenly stops going forward. You sail over the handlebars don't you? Correct, bike stops, he doesn't. At high tide the water is only 3-4 meters from the top of the white boat-fixing upstand. You guessed it, the tide was out! Over 10 meters he dropped, landing flat on his back in about ½ meter of muddy water. His flight would have had a much softer landing if the tide had been in but there would have been an issue with that. He couldn't swim!
Winded but amazingly with no other injuries I retrieved him from the mud and we made a slow and bedraggled trudge back to his house where I rang the doorbell and explained what had happened. His Mum was not impressed. To this day he still can't swim.

John Court

Shells and bombs galore

I was born in Edinburgh in 1947. My Dad was a builder and he formed a self-build group in an area in the south of the city. Edinburgh is the capital of Scotland but is also a garrison city with Dreghorn and Redford Barracks and of course Edinburgh Castle. To the rear of our house was the married quarter's for Redford Barracks and beyond that were woods and then farmland and on the lower reaches of the Pentland hills was Swanston Golf Club. To the east of that was the military firing range where the recruits practiced.

One day during the Easter holidays my two friends Roger and Alistair and I decided we were going to collect brass 303 bullet cases. We were all around 10 years of age and didn't have a care in the world. I remember it was an ideal spring day. We had gas mask holders which we used as school satchels to put our finds in. As ten year olds we understood that if the red flag was flying at the entrance to the range we were not allowed in as it was too dangerous, what it actually meant was do not enter under any circumstances as live ammo was being used. There was a green flag flying so no danger we thought. This was WD (War Department) property and no one was allowed in. We ignored this and walked up to the range and there was no one in sight. We found loads of cases and soon filled our bags.

After a while we saw an old 2nd world war tank half way up a hill behind the range. We walked up to it and it was obviously a target for mortars or small cannons. It was smashed up pretty badly. We looked all around the tank. At this point I should point out that there was not a soul in sight.

There were loads of rabbit holes around and I saw the tail of a mortar bomb sticking out of a rabbit hole. Before going on Easter holiday we were reminded by our teacher that we would have to write an essay on what we did on our break. Anyway I picked the bomb up and after we examined it I put it in my bag.

We decided not to tell anyone about the item and that I would take to school after the holidays. I also decided not to tell my parents or even my brother about the bomb. I hid the bomb in the outside shed.

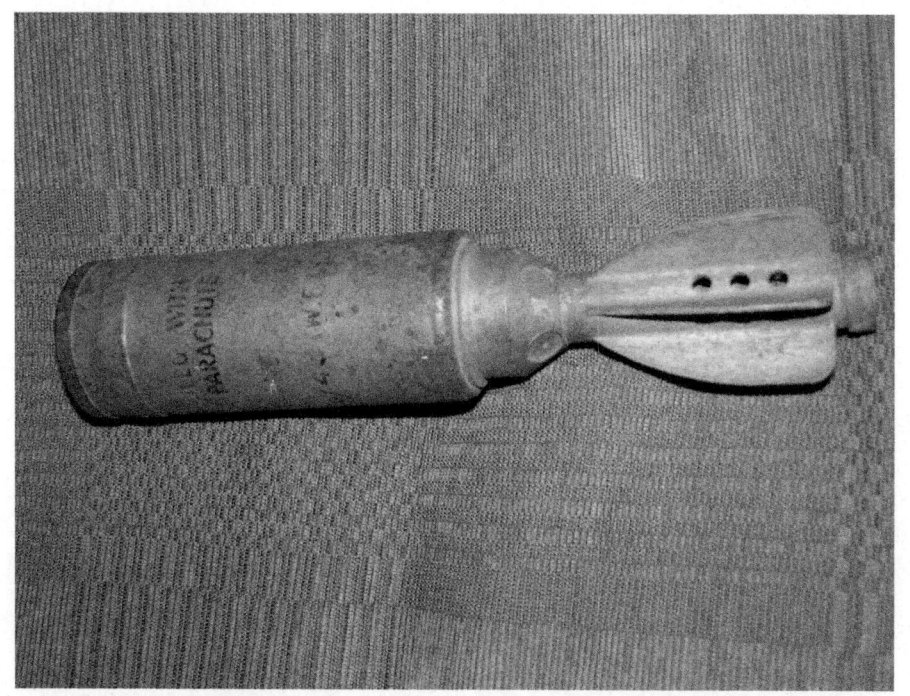

I took it to school a few days later and showed it to all my schoolmates before class. When our teacher Ms Tanner asked if anyone had done anything exciting on holiday I put my hand up. She told me to come out to the front of the class and show what I had in my bag. When I opened my satchel she let out an involuntary scream and told me to put the bomb on her desk and calmly told us to get into the playground. I just shrugged my shoulders as did Roger and Alistair. The next minute all hell broke loose. There were fire engines, police and soon after bomb disposal officers arrived. When the dust settled I / we got a good dressing down and were sent home. Needless to say we never went anywhere the ranges again.

MR MEL LOCKETT

Stuart Gillies

Scorched Earth

Back in 1952 in the sleepy little seaside town of Littlehampton on the West Sussex coast I was one of a group of boys around 10 years of age who played regularly together. I remember particularly one game we used to play that was quite scary when you think about it and certainly would be considered irresponsible today. We used to go out into the fields not far from our homes with a box of matches and "play" the following game!! We would all light a patch of grass and then see who could wait the longest before putting the fire out just by stamping on it.

There were a number of occasions when things almost got out of hand with several fires nearly out of control. On one occasion the fires were raging so much that we thought that we might have to call the fire brigade. Fortunately with a few 'hot feet' we managed to get control back so the fire brigade was not needed. When we got back home our parents wanted to know why our hair and eyebrows were singed!!

Peter Smith

Introduction to gardening and swearing

I was born in the Mayday Hospital in Croydon 1943 but my brother Malcolm was actually born at home (I have no idea why) but I clearly remember, even at just three years old being taken into my parents' bedroom to meet my brother. By now the whole family are living in Fernhurst Road, Addiscombe, Croydon. We had quite a long garden and I was always keen to "help" Dad with bits and pieces until I was much older and he started to teach me how to sow seed, plant things out and then one day when cleaning the lawn mower, the old push type of course, he managed a deep cut in one of his fingers which required a hospital visit and several stitches. The following day he wondered if under supervision I could finish the mowing. This was like promotion to me so I gladly took the job on; the funny thing is it then became my weekly job! I also remember Dad picking runner beans in the summer when he accidentally broke one of the stems "f--k it" he said. The first time I heard my Dad swear. I can't remember the reason but in the kitchen with my Mum sometime later I myself uttered those magic words "f--k it" I said, which achieved a serious clip round the ear from her. "Why? Dad said it" amazing when you think there was also a "blimey" box which had to receive a penny 'donation' from our pocket money every time that word was used! My Nanny & Grandad lived in Freemasons Road, Lower Addiscombe with the East Croydon to London railway line at the bottom of a long narrow garden which was tended to by Grandad growing all sorts of vegetables, with tomatoes in his greenhouse, which he built himself, so my interest in gardening was directly down my to Dad & Grandad. At the bottom of Grandad's garden almost under the railway he had an impromptu shed in which he bred rabbits but looking back they were not kept as pets! Outside the back door of the house was a separate building always known as 'the bungalow' was principally Nanny's laundry - no washing machines in those days - just a huge sink, a washing line outside and a massive cast iron mangle. NB There are still about a dozen houses left in Freemasons Road, a block of flats took the rest, so their house and garden are still visible as you leave East Croydon on the way to Victoria.

Ray Fry

W. H. Rhodes Trust Trip to Canada 1959

In 1958, I was Head Boy of King Edward Sixth Camp Hill, Grammar School Birmingham. A week after being appointed, I was called into the Heads study. Mr Rogers was a severe serious Quaker who took no prisoners. I went in worrying about what I may have done wrong as Head of Prefects. I stood at his desk and waited. He looked up from some papers and said "Williams, you will be pleased to hear that you are one of eight boys selected from Birmingham to get a Rhodes Trust Scholarship for six weeks to Eastern Canada next Summer. Congratulations and make the most of the opportunity. Mr Bates, Deputy Head will give you all the details." With that, I was ushered out of his study. I staggered down the corridor in a daze.

It turned out that a multi-millionaire from Bradford had visited Canada and was so impressed by its potential that he arranged to pay for forty eight senior boys from top schools in the UK to visit Canada every other year or so. He had made his money initially after he had the idea of providing an overall cleaning service for Northern factories. He had then expanded by setting up a whole Chain of high end China and pottery shops.

The eight boys from Brum had to meet regularly with the accompanying master for the rest of the school year to learn about Canada (including being able to sing their national anthem) prepare to present a show to passengers on the ship and be able to give talks on our own home area.

Mike is on the left.

In July 1959, we finally travelled by train to Liverpool, decked out in our red and gold striped ties with Canadian maple leaf shields. There we met with all the rest of the group, including sixteen boys from London, eight from Manchester, eight from Leeds/Bradford with the eight from Glasgow joining us at Greenock. Air flights were less used in those days, so we were to travel by Cunard on the Carinthia, with a mixture of steerage and first class privileges. The ship was a place of wonder to eighteen year old boys most of whom, like me, had never seen luxury like it. We ate first class occasionally. The menu was the size of an atlas and I had never seen so much cutlery. We mixed with very wealthy passengers, including quite a few stunning daughters! We had to give a show on board. Fortunately, there were quite a few talented lads amongst us, including two brilliant pianists, one classical, one jazz. We had a Scots piper of course and some very good singers and actors, so it all went well.

On arriving at Greenock, loads of passengers came on board by tender who were emigrating. Many were tearful at seeing their homeland for the last time in many years. Imagine then the effect when the Carinthia got ready to leave. The last tender pulled away and a lone piper in full highland dress appeared on its top deck and played, "Will ye 'no come back again", as we sailed regally down the Clyde. People were sobbing all over the place.

Once clear of Scotland, we discovered that a force ten in the North Irish Sea was no respecter of size as we tossed about like a toy boat. Later it got calmer and we enjoyed watching flying fish dart round the ship. Our first sight of Canada was Belle isle strait off Newfoundland. We then proceeded down the hugely wide St Lawrence River past beautiful forests, waterfalls and mountains.

We eventually made our first port of call in Quebec. So French it hurt. Charles de Gaulle, the French President had really upset the Canadian government by calling for a Québec libre, on his visit and had promptly been asked to leave, so the Québécois were not that keen to welcome the English.

None the less I loved the place. Despite my nervousness at having to do a thank you to the mayor of Quebec in French, I found the old quarter lovely. The heights of Abraham are fantastic, the cathedral was beautifully decorated. Lunch at the Chateau Frontenac was special.

Then it was off to Montreal. This was a very exciting place with all the signs in two languages. The French spoken had quite a few differences from France French, especially in accent and vocabulary. I will always remember them stunning night-time view over the city from Mont Royale itself. No underground shopping centres then of course. Next we went to the capital Ottawa. Nice enough place but the Parliament and museum tours did not do a lot for me.

Our final port of call was Toronto. Here after a spectacular sail under the Jacques Cartier Bridge we disembarked into a very posh five star hotel called the King Edward. The famous longest road in the world started near there, called Yonge or Young street or something like that. We were very lucky to arrive as the World Trade Fair opened on the island in the middle of Toronto. It was amazingly diverse in terms of exhibitions from all over the planet. We had tickets for the opening night as well where I remember John Kerr of South Pacific fame singing. A famous American comedian starred too but his name eludes me. We went the newly opened (by her Majesty) Queen Elizabeth highway. Then it was onto Niagara Falls. On the way we passed through St Catherine's, one of the prettiest places you could ever wish to live.

Hamilton on the other hand was hot and sticky, though McMaster University was another place I would love to have studied.

We did all the usual tourist things at Niagara. I found the museum of craft that people had gone over the falls in (and mostly survived), fascinating. Being me, I could not resist walking over the Rainbow Bridge leading into the USA, so I could say I'd been there. A burly Buffalo State cop escorted me at speed back over the bridge to Canada, making it clear that I was lucky not to be arrested and formally deported.

One disappointment was when I purchased a stick of Niagara printed rock for my little sister only to discover afterwards it had " made in Blackpool UK " printed on the inside.

The next part of the tour was in many ways the best. We were taken to the railway station at Toronto where we boarded the Canadian Pacific sleeper, ultimate destination BC. The cabins were full of all sorts of gadgets which opened and closed things. You did not have time to sleep.

We got out at North Bay near Lake Huron. Way out in the middle of nowhere. We were coached through vast forests to

Sudbury which turned out to be a real shock. The town was the headquarters of INCO, the centre of the mining industry in Canada for zinc copper aluminium and nickel. The place stank of sulphur and was mostly coloured brown and yellow with few trees. They tell me it has changed radically now, but despite the mines being really interesting, we could not wait to get out of the place,

We then had the best week of our holiday. We were taken by boat (The only way in, other than sea plane) to the Lakes of Temagami and Wanapitai far out in the forest wilderness, miles from any sign of civilisation. The lakes were so clear you just drank that water untreated. We were put up in log cabins by the lake. We fished, game-watched, swam, Canadian canoed, walked and stargazed for a whole week. It was paradise. The presence of fifty Canadian girl students of our age, camping nearby, was a great bonus of course. Strict segregation regulations were in force and enforced but we had a great time. I learned in later years that several permanent relationships started there. One girl I met said she was intending to make it as a film star. I think she did.

Going back to civilisation was hard but the return ship Sylvania made the journey very pleasant. I arrived home to learn that I had been given a place at

Sheffield University so no time to get bored.

Mike Williams

Case Closed!

Casting my mind back to 1979 I can see myself as a fine 23 year old lad with no moral compass... ahh those were the days... now sadly long gone! My story is about Sue. Quite how I met Sue is another story, worthy of being told but for the risk of exposing the teller as a Cad. Anyway, suffice to say, Sue and I were mutually attracted, but not really an 'item'... (it was complicated) but we did enjoy sharing the same sheets when possible! On this particular occasion she invited me to her flat for dinner. It was my first, and subsequently last, visit to her posh pad in St John's wood, London. Whilst the invitation was for dinner, I had read between the lines and prepared myself with an overnight bag, but felt it a tad forward to arrive on the doorstep bag in hand.

Wisdom suggested that I leave it in the car and replace it with a bottle of wine... good call! I don't remember which floor her flat was on, but I do recall that it was number 11. I would have arrived late, on account that I have never knowingly arrived early for anything! A warm invitation greeted me and soon the bottle of wind had gone and been replaced by another. I'm sure that the dinner was delicious but in reality I saw it as no more than foreplay to the main serving that would come! Time passed very quickly and soon it was time to address the elephant in the room... to stay or not to stay. Bingo... the offer was forthcoming and the need for an overnight bag became a reality. So whilst Sue slipped into the bathroom to freshen up and don something a little more revealing, I decided to pop down to the car and collect my things. I left her door on ajar and took the lift to the ground floor where I wedged the front door open for my return access.

It didn't take long to sprint to the car, grab my bag and make my way back to the lift. I hit the button; the doors closed and as the compartment rose as did my excitement! 3 flats per floor would make it floor 3, or was it floor 4, no matter, the lift doors opened and I went to her flat door which she had closed. I rang the bell and waited. Perhaps she was still in the bathroom or couldn't hear it, so I pressed the button again but this time held it down so that there could be no mistake... Buzzzzzzzz At this point dear reader, I want you to imagine the sound of a voice from a really frail old lady with a distinctive quiver, because that is the voice that came from behind the door... "Who'sssss that"? the voice came. Oh goodie I thought, Sue's a real laugh, I like this game! With that I conjured up the deepest, darkest and most scary voice that I could muster... something similar as that which I would imagine greeted Little Red Riding Hood when the evil wolf expressed his wish to gobble her up. "It's me. Let me in" I growled as I banged upon the door. "Gowwww away" the little voice pleaded. Oh this was fun I thought. The night was young and already we were into roll play! The letterboxes in these 1930's doors were large. Large enough for me to put my entire forearm through and start waving my wrist looking for something to grab, whilst at the same time upping the ante with the door banging and menacing voice. The little voice now turned to a scream which started to raise alarm bells in my tiny brain.

At this point my eyes suddenly focused on the door number... Oh My God, I thought, I've got the wrong flat! Time to make a quick apology and do a runner! By the time I got to Sue's flat, with the door still ajar, my libido was rapidly diminishing with the thought of the poor old lady upstairs. I recanted my tail to Sue and she agreed that she would explain the mistake to the old lady in the morning and hopefully put things right.

We were just discussing the explanation when her doorbell rang. PC Plod and his able assistant was standing outside asking us if we had seen anything suspicious in the apartments as there had been an "incident"! The guilt in my face led to the quickest confession our esteemed establishment has ever extracted, and soon both PC's were rolling around on the floor in laughter...

case closed!

Adrian Beal

VE Day 8th May – or is it?

I believe that I am the only living soul who knows that it is, in fact, not the 8th but the 7th. As a lad I was always disappointed that my Dad never talked about the war. I wanted plenty of, preferably violent, reminiscences of daring do.

However, one story he proudly told me was; how he single handedly won the war with a few flicks of his index finger! For some weeks before war's end it was apparent that victory wasn't far away. A substantial number of servicemen started a "book"; the betting type, on what day the war would actually end. My Dad chose his birthday - 8th May.

At this time my Dad was head of communications of a department at the SOE. He received messages, coded them up, and sent them off to front line forces by Morse code where they would be decoded and actioned.

Late in the evening of the 7 May 1945 my dad, Norman Robertson received the long-awaited message from the war office which simply stated.

'Hostilities to cease with immediate effect – victory in Europe'.

With this new message in his grubby paws, he decided to adjourn to the mess and enjoy a few beers. He waited until five minutes past midnight, before he duly tapped away his Morse code message. And so he ended the war with a few taps of his immortal, or should I say immoral, digit and was able to claim on a tidy bet.

Malcolm Robertson

A Jimmy Greaves memory

As a young teenager, my brother Geoff and I, along with three mates, used to deliver the newspapers throughout Pevensey, Pevensey Bay, Normans Bay, Westham, Stone Cross and Hankham. We received minimal pocket money per week, and the pay for the paper rounds was not very much either. However, that was all quite normal in the 1950s.

There was no such thing as football being shown on television in those days. In fact in the road I lived in, Hobney Rise, Westham, which is a part of a small council estate, there was only one television, and the only football match shown back then, was the FA cup final. We would all save our pocket money and paper money for a few weeks, and then go to watch a football match, in the Football League, Division 1, (Forerunner to the Premier League).

We went to all the London grounds at one time or another, and in 1957, Portsmouth were in Division 1 and we went several times to matches there. We would do our paper rounds on match days, which back then, were only on Saturdays, go to the Pevensey & Westham railway station, buy our tickets, which cost around twelve shillings for a return ticket, then travel up to London, or to Portsmouth, changing trains at Brighton. In London, we would travel by the underground from Victoria, and I'm pretty certain that the train from Brighton to Portsmouth, stopped at Fratton in Portsmouth, the station being a fairly short walk to Fratton Park, the Portsmouth football club stadium, which is still in use today.

In the 1950's, the pitch was surrounded by a wall, separating it from the terraces and grandstands. The front of the terracing was some four feet below this wall and the pitch was about a foot below it. In the 50s, youngsters like us, would always be shepherded down to stand immediately behind the wall, so that we could see.

On Boxing Day, 1957, we went to Fratton Park, to watch Portsmouth play against Chelsea. We were immediately opposite the centre line of the pitch, with our chins either resting on, or just above the previously mentioned wall.

At the kick off, Jimmy Greaves was just about to start the game, when my brother hauled himself up the wall, onto the top of it, and ran across to Greavesie, shouting 'Mr Greaves, please sign my programme' (Cost 3d). Greavesie gestured to the referee to wait a minute; he took Geoff's programme, signed it, patted him on the head and sent him on his way back to us.

Geoff was the youngest of us, being 13 at the time of this match. Can you imagine the current prima donnas ever doing anything like that, if it was even possible to be able to get within touching distance of them? Portsmouth won that day, 3 – 0, so it was a rare day that Jimmy Greaves didn't score. Around three months ago, Jan and I were taking our daughter's Springer Spaniel for a walk towards the harbour, when we saw one of the guys who had been at Portsmouth on that day. We got chatting about various things, and he asked me how my brother was. Geoff died three years ago, and when I told the guy, Mick King, he said to me "I will always remember that Boxing Day we were at Portsmouth to watch Portsmouth play Chelsea, and Geoff ran across the pitch, just as the match was about to start, to get his programme signed by Greavesie, and Greavesie did it, didn't he?"

As the old adage goes 'Happy days'.

Paul Roberts

Winning the Lottery (in reverse)!

In many ways I have been the luckiest chap on earth, and whilst I have never felt that I deserve such good fortune, I do try to remember each day how blessed I am, and appreciate my good luck. However, luck is not always around and sometimes she deserts us altogether. I think upon reading this story you will agree that on this particular occasion at least, she was definitely plotting against me!

I shall cast my mind back to 1982 and a time when I had just moved to London, leaving my girlfriend in Eastbourne but returning every weekend to cement our relationship in the only way that youngsters can! It was summer, a time when beautiful young girls would roam about on hot days wearing very little. Pubs were open until late, the evenings long and barmy, and the chance of finding 'love' high!

And so it was on this particular evening when opportunity came knocking whist queuing for a Kebab in the local takeaway. I was living in a shared house with a young 'couple' and was very much the odd one out, which meant that a pint or two at the 'Crooked Billet' on Wimbledon Common, followed by a takeaway, had become the 'norm'.

My girlfriend had just taken a summer job on a live-aboard boat traveling the Rhine in Germany so as far as I was concerned I had a 'get out of jail' card and was hell-bent on breaking the rules!

So, back to the greasy kebab shop and the queue…. There are probably 5 or 6 people ahead of me, all eager to stuff some cheap meat and soggy chips down their gullets, after a session of late night drinking. But the difference this night was that there was more on the menu than just grub… stood in front of me was a rather attractive girl in a short dress. At first I tried not to notice having assumed that the lucky man next to her was the other half of the whole. But as the queue slowly moved forward I couldn't help noticing that there was no eye contact or words exchanged between them, and in fact I was the lucky man because it was to me that she spoke.

Given that all of a sudden the queue seemed to be moving far too quickly and my time to strike diminishing rapidly, I had to act fast. At the time I had just got my first 'proper' job which included a brand new company car and pile of business cards proudly displayed the fact that I was a 'Sales Executive'. Having your first business card certainly makes a young man feel very important, especially if it contained the word "Executive"… surely a title that could only be trumped by the words "Chief Executive"! In reality the purpose of a business card was considered by my company as a tool to gain new customers and thus progressing the opportunities of shifting some dodgy stock, but to me these cards were much more about the opportunity they gave to impress the opposite sex, which was a damn sight easier that getting new customers!

Anyway, back to the diminishing queue… time was running out so I asked the girl if she fancied going out for a drink one evening. To my surprise she seemed very keen on the idea, and was genuinely apologetic that she was going away for a month, but promised to call me when she returned. I admit that it was a little disheartening that I would have to wait, but I willingly proffered a new business card and told her that I would look forward to her phone call. That was it really… nothing more, just an innocent chat in a greasy takeaway and a future opportunity of losing my innocence!

Life would go on as normal… or so I thought! Now at this point you may be wondering why I chose the title of this story, and when you find out you are not going to believe it. However, it is true despite the chances of it happening being so remote that it makes winning the Euro Lottery a "dead cert" in comparison…

We didn't have mobile phones in those days, so calls to

our beloved were planned, either she would call you at a predetermined time or you would call her on a particular day. Either way one would stand by the phone at the allotted time and share love and affection down a crackly line for as short a period as was necessary. The weekend arrived along with the promised phone call from a pay phone somewhere deep inside Germany that would carry the seductive tones of a loved-up girlfriend missing the man of her dreams.

But to my horror the conversation didn't quite go to script, indeed it went something like this:

"Hi darling."

"Hi."
"Missing you. How are things on the boat?"

"Are you?"

"Yes of course… why?"

"I've got a new room-mate."

"Excellent, is she nice?"

"You tell me!"

"What do you mean?"

"We have just been chatting and I was telling her all about you. Then she started telling me about this new bloke that she has just met and how she is looking forward to seeing him when she gets back to London."

"Yes… so?"

"So she hands me your business card you plonker!"

"Sh*t… I can explain…"

"Don't bother!"

The call ended abruptly, along with my dreams of marriage and children (NOT!), furthermore I never received that promised phone call and neither did I win the lottery!

Adrian Beal

Latch Door Kids

OK, let's get a bit crude shall we?
You will have heard the phrase 'Latch Door Kids' which refers to children coming home from school to an empty house, with both or sometimes the only, parent being at work, get their own meal and then disappear outside with little or no parental guidance.
My story has a little twist on this and in some ways is similar to the 'knock and run' stories others have mentioned. I lived in an area of Sheffield that had a mixture of modern housing estates (1930s) and old back to back or terraced houses. Many of the latter had their one and only khazi (toilet) at the bottom of the garden. Most doors, whether the front or back of the house, and the khazi had thumb latches.

The game some of my friends played; I hasten to add, I was not involved; was to put a drawing pin on the thumb latch so when someone came to use it they would press down on the drawing pin with their thumb. However, In order to stop the drawing pin falling off the thumb latch it would be held in place by a piece of, wait for it, 'dog S..t,' the stickier the better. I know you are already ahead of me! Going down to the khazi, when it had gone dark, for a final visit just before bed, the unassuming victim, already leaving their need until the very last minute so he/she would not have to spend too much time in the cold, would put their thumb over the latch, press down, yell ouch! and immediately put their thumb into their mouth!!!!!
I did warn you it was crude!

Mel Lockett

CHAPTER 3 – EDUCATION

◆ ◆ ◆

'Brown bread was something only poor people ate'

◆ ◆ ◆

'Oil was for lubricating, fat was for cooking'

◆ ◆ ◆

'Tea was made in a teapot with brown leaves. It was never green'

◆ ◆ ◆

'Rice was a pudding and never part of a main course'

Mingling with sporting greats!

With my GCE's compete and 'A' level grades good enough, I was off to Loughborough University. Loughborough is famous for two age old courses, PE teaching and Handicraft (later Design technology) teachers. PE students are 'jocks' (work it out) and the practical students (me) are 'chippies'. The year is 1973 when a naïve Manx student arrives in Loughborough.

On the Saturday after arrival, I go down to investigate the market town and I am absolutely shocked to be addressed as 'me duck'. 'Alright me duck' could be heard everywhere. What had I come to?

Now Loughborough is a place for elite sport and training.

Alongside me were Dave Moorcroft and Sebastian Coe. Both in my year group and both (apparently) on the same four year teaching course as I.

Dave Moorcroft (middle distance UK international and former 5,000 metres World record holder) and Seb Coe (now His Lordship! with more achievements than I can list) received the same degree on the same day as I, but I'm not bitter. His Lordship trained very hard but I never saw him in a lecture or eating the same food in the refectory along with the rest of us mortals. Dave Moorcroft was more visible and I guess appeared for about half of the course. Both were out of sight and often the country when international duty called. They even had minders.

Loughborough was used as a centre for international team training. This was in the days of England Rugby players not being fully professional. The England squad would arrive on the campus on a Friday for a weekend training camp. On Saturday evenings after thrashing the University First 15 they would assemble in the bar to continue their squad training. I recall Bill Beaumont and his team mates sitting in a line on the bar floor having boat races for many hours. For those who think that this is a reference to physical fitness on rowing machines think again. It requires two teams sitting in lines alongside each other with each member holding a full pint of beer. On the instruction to start, number one on both sides downs his pint as quickly as possible and demonstrates his success by placing the glass on top of his head. Number 2 can now begin and repeat until the end of the line signifies a winning team. This relay would be repeated 5 or 6 times a night until a new game was initiated. Training for England internationals must be different today I guess. Or is it?

John Court

CHAPTER 4 – MOTORING

◆ ◆ ◆

'Coffee was Camp and came in a bottle'

◆ ◆ ◆

'Only Heinz made beans'

◆ ◆ ◆

'Chilli meant it was cold outside'

◆ ◆ ◆

'Prunes were medicinal'

Pirelli Stamp

As a lad growing up on Hayling Island in the 1950s, I used to help Dad in the garden and listen to the sounds of the motorbikes as they passed the other side of the high hedge that screened our house from the road. It got so that I could recognise the make of bike by the sound of the engine, easily differentiating between Greeves, Norton's, Velocette's, Triumphs, BSA and others. Finally, in 1961, the day arrived when I was old enough to have a motorbike of my own. A pal, older than me, was selling his first bike for £12 and I needed no persuasion to buy it. As a first year engineering apprentice with a weekly income of £2.16s.8d, (£2.86) this was a major expenditure and though I had enough money to buy the obligatory crash helmet; boots and leathers would have to wait.

The bike, a 125cc James scrambler, was dented, rusty, and had clearly been well scrambled, but to me it was a two wheeled beauty.

My first ride took me on to a dual carriageway. I was proudly riding in the inside lane, no doubt grinning from ear to ear, when the vehicles in front stopped at some traffic lights.

I glided to a halt behind a car and lent over to put my right foot down, only to find that the kick-start lever had gone up my flapping trouser leg, preventing my foot from reaching the ground. I sprawled full length on the road, a bit like Del Boy leaning on the non-existent bar counter. As I fell my right hand was extended to save myself. At the same moment a big six cylinder Vauxhall Velux (they don't make 'em like that these days) in the outside lane eased forward in the traffic queue so that its rear wheel was parked on top of my hand. I feared that the Velux driver might be in a hurry and a wheel spin start would have been the end of my hand. Fortunately other motorists saw my plight and four of them managed to lift the car sufficiently for me to get my hand free. Surprisingly, other than my pride, some bruising and a Pirelli imprint on the back of my hand, I sustained no serious injury though to this day I am sure that the incident is to blame for every bad golf shot that I hit. Boots and leathers were still not affordable but I managed to solve the trouser leg problem by purchasing army gaiters from a government surplus shop, price 2s 6d. (12.5p) No photographs of this Knight of the Road exist … thank God.

Barry Alford

Smog

I can hardly believe it now but as close as the mid-1960s we still had bouts of smog. Smog is a mixture of fog and the smoke output from domestic fires and industrial chimneys. Up in Stalybridge (Greater Manchester) the northern town where I was born, the smog was often so bad you literally could not see more than about six feet (in old money) in front of you. That did not stop us from going out to play. On the contrary, there was fun to be had.

Sometimes it was so bad that the local council would go around placing oil-burning lamps on the street corners to warn where the kerbside was and which direction the road was going. These lamps would give off an eerie yellow glow with the smoke they produced not exactly helping to improve the already smog-filled air! Our game, if you have not already guessed it was to have a great time moving those lamps all over the place. We would only scarper when we had at least got a bus to turn up the wrong street. After our escapades were completed we would then be homeward bound, safe in the knowledge that the fuming bus driver and conductor had no idea where we lived thanks to the camouflage capabilities of the smog!

Graham Shaw

It's in the post

Back in the days before the 'breathalyser', it was not uncommon to drive home after an away fixture having graciously accepted the hospitality of the home team. Whilst there was no legal drinking limit, the police could take action if they suspected over-indulgence. On one occasion, I was one of four passengers in a 2-seater sports car. The driver, the fifth occupant in the car, shall we say, had to concentrate very hard. Unfortunately, he was stopped by a police car. Thankfully, the driver was not asked to step out of the car (he would not have been able to stand up) but was asked if he was aware that one of his rear lights was not working. The driver replied "It's in the post" (the usual excuse for having an out of date tax disc). The police officer asked if we had far to go and suggested that the driver take care.

Tony Uden

Leaks for a Fiver!

As a young man of 17 back in 1969 having just passed my driving test I was keen to become a vehicle owner, my wages as an apprentice electrician was at that time approx. £6.2s.6d (£6.125p) for a 40 hour week, so my price range for a car purchase wasn't great, however through scouring the local paper I found what I thought what would be the perfect purchase and a bargain. Having contacted the owner and arranged a viewing off I went with my total savings of £35.00 the asking price for the vehicle was £40.00. The prospective car was a very old VW beetle, the negotiation was a tough one the owner not willing to drop his price to my £35.00 but we did agree on me paying the £35.00 there and then with a further £5.00 to be paid in two weeks' time when hopefully I will have saved the outstanding monies.

I drove off the proud owner of this very old VW complete with 6 volt electrics so very dim headlights, very small oval rear window and no fuel gauge just a small lever at floor level to bring in the reserve tank if required. All went well for the first few days until it rained then I discovered that water flowed into the front floor pan through the heating vents almost causing the need for wellington boots.

This caused me to rethink the payment of the outstanding £5.00 and thought he could whistle for it, feeling confident that he wouldn't have the cheek to chase me for it. Meanwhile being of an engineering background I set about finding a solution to the water issue, my solution was to drill holes in the rear floor pan of the car hence causing a flow in at the front and out at the rear, whilst not being the most of elegant of solutions it seemed to work. All was well for a further two weeks until whilst I parked the car out the front of a house I was cutting the lawn for, (part time job to earn a bit more cash), when round the corner of the house into the back garden came the previous owner of the car demanding the outstanding £5.00, needless to say the conversation got very heated and threatening, but what he hadn't taken into consideration was the house owner, who was a lady of, shall we say, a well-built nature in her late fifties. She suddenly appeared at the back door having heard the commotion; she was not one to be messed with and immediately leapt to my defence giving him a very strong point of view!!! His disappeared back around the corner of the house with his tail between his legs never to be seen again, needless to say I never did pay the outstanding £5.00!!!

Dave Burnett

Mini Bang! Bang!

In 1972, after years of driving bangers and rust buckets, I bought my first brand new car. It was a beige coloured mini. It was a thing of beauty and at £700, and a major dent in my pocket. On the third day of ownership I drove the car to work. I stopped at a pedestrian crossing and glancing in my rear view mirror, I was horrified to see that the large car behind me showed no sign of stopping. The impact was severe, with the boot lid, bumper and surrounding panels all distorted. I confronted the driver of the car. He had a pencil behind his ear and a crossword puzzle on the dashboard. He said he was dazzled by the light. Did I mention that it was raining?

That evening I stood outside the house forlornly surveying the damage. A car came round the corner, and as it did so, the passenger door swung open and the driver ducked down below the dashboard. I had to stand and watch as the car ploughed into the front of my mini. The driver, a woman, explained that the passenger door had not been shut properly, and her handbag, on the passenger seat, had slid towards the open door. She had of course felt an irresistible urge to rescue it! Both ends of my beautiful vehicle having been stoved in, I had started the day with a mini and finished with a min.

Barry Alford

Summer of 1955 – First Family Holiday

It is July 1955 leading up to the six week summer school break. I am seven years old. My Dad, Bernard, having passed his driving test a few months previously was now the proud owner of a two door Morris 8 (our first family car).

My Mum, Margaret, decides we should have our first family holiday so informs Dad he would be driving us to Cullompton, Devon where she had been evacuated during the war. Preparation for the journey included, spare bottles of water as the car radiator used to boil dry, a tin of ready rolled and prepared Old Holborn cigarettes (Dad was a heavy smoker and need them for the journey), a tin (no Tupperware in those days) of prepared sandwiches, egg & Cress/Spam and pickle. Also, a small methylated spirit camping stove, kettle, tea pot, and plastic cups and saucers and one large leather suitcase with all the family clothes in.

Early August and the journey planned, map books and itinerary all on Mums lap on the front seat. Our suitcase strapped on the back of the car along with the spare wheel. Dad fidgety and keen to get underway after consuming three cups of tea (his usual breakfast along with two Old Holborn roll – ups). Mum ushering Anne, my sister aged four, and me into the back of the tiny new family limousine!! 6.00 am in the morning, Beltring Road, Eastbourne, all quiet, sleep still in my eyes and moaning about having to go so early. Off we go on our two-hundred-mile trek. No dual carriageways, motorways or any other fast roads in those days. Very few towns or city by-passes so negotiating each town or village would be an obstacle for our little 850cc carriage. Very soon the first obstacle: Lewes, the High Street, a hump-back bridge and a steep hill. The jalopy just about made it, first stop to top up the radiator. This was to continue, stop start – stop start for the whole journey.

One longstop just past Portsmouth and we had our sandwiches and a pot of tea. Dad nearly set himself on fire by spilling methylated spirits on his arm which he had to put out quickly by plunging his arm into a ditch close by. No injury caused thank goodness. Drama over, we continued on with Mum navigating, Dad moaning and smoking whilst driving. My little sister fast asleep, is laying her legs and feet across my side of the cramped back seat. Eleven hot and sweaty tiring hours later we arrived at a small terraced house which would be our B & B for the next fortnight. The holiday was a great success, visiting local farms owned by a Mr & Mrs Baisley, great cooked breakfasts and cream teas. My memory recalls the fact that in those days school summer breaks were always hot & sunny, the pace of living so much slower and simple things like playing marbles or collecting cigarette cards were uncomplicated and pleasurable pass-times. Are these memories real? The journey home was just as arduous but the memory of that first big family holiday still sticks with me warmly. Thank you Mum and Dad you got us back safe and sound.

John Maynard

A hill too much

John Maynard's wonderful story reminds me of 1955 and a week Youth Hostelling in The North East and Yorkshire. It was Easter and myself and two pals made it by train from Sheffield to Saltburn-by-the-Sea on Easter Saturday and promptly made it to the Youth Hostel, sadly no longer a YHA but a private house.

We booked in and collected, for the princely sum of 1/6d (7.5p) a cotton sleeping bag each. Unfortunately we could not book in for the Sunday night as the hostel was full. Problem!

We then quickly made it down to the beach via one of the world's oldest water-powered funiculars. Well worth a visit.

We were fortunate to meet some older teenagers; I was 15 and my pals 16; who told us they were camping on the other side of the valley and why didn't we oin them. We met up with them later that evening and they lent us a sleeping bag each. We spent the night sleeping, or at least trying to, under the stars. Yes, in Saltburn-by-the-Sea, Easter 1955, we slept under the stars.

We were able to get back into the Youth Hostel for Easter Monday, and another 1/6d, before setting off south.

We stayed at YHA places in Whitby - The hostel used to be in a long red bricked building at the top of the famous 199 steps up to the Bram Stokers Whitby Abbey.

Robin Hoods Bay – or rather Boggle Hole YHA situated in a creek ½ mile south and thankfully still there as a Youth Hostel but also given a three star hotel rating.

Our next stop was to be Scarborough, a good 15 mile hike south. However, after about four miles we managed to thumb a lift. This is where John's story kicks in and why this is in the 'Motoring' section. An elderly couple; well to us teenagers they were elderly, but probably in their 60s; took pity on us and pulled up in their Austin 7, similar to the photo in John's story. Somehow we managed to get three teenagers with their large ex-army ruck-sacks into the back seat and off we went on a rather hairy but enjoyable lift to Scarborough.

We entered Scarborough via the Peasholm Park end, and proceeded on to the North Beach road. A few hundred yards south on there is a turning into Albert Road which leads up the hillside via a very sharp right hand corner to the hotels at the top. The couple need to go up there to get to their hotel. Unfortunately the little old Austin 7 with five passengers and three rucksacks could not make it. It ground to a halt. The three of us got out of the car with our gear and had to give the car a push to start it off again. We shouted our thanks to the couple as the car disappeared round the bend never to be seen again.

I remember this as a great holiday being our first freedom from parents. I also remember we got our train tickets back to Sheffield from Scarborough leaving us with just enough money to catch the tram home when we got there.

Mel Lockett

Wolseley Outriders

Back in the day, July 1965 to be precise, a few friends and I decided that on this particular evening we would take a trip out to a relatively local country Pub. At the time my father had bought me my first motor car as I had recently passed my driving test.

The car was an old Wolseley 18 saloon. It had two huge isolated head lamps and 2 indicators that popped out at each side of the car like a couple of small wings. The upholstery was old leather and looked magnificent. The car also had running boards (one on either side of the car). These were to prove very useful.

The Pub we would be heading for was The High Rocks Inn, on the outskirts of Tunbridge Wells and as we all lived on the Ramslye Estate in Tunbridge Wells, it was about 5 or 6 miles away. Back then the Pub was associated with the High Rocks Outdoor Climbing facility and was once used in the filming of Robin Hood. Nowadays, the Pub describes the route as down a quiet country lane. In 1965 it was a forest. There were six of us making the journey, all aged between 17 and 18. We set off travelling across the forest. Arriving safely, we proceeded to enjoy our night out, which of course we did.

Come closing time and on leaving the Pub we were horrified to have stepped out into thick fog. It was a real peasouper with visibility down to about 9 or 10 yards. How were we to get home? Somebody came up with the idea of having the driver and three passengers on the inside and 2 outriders, 1 on either side of the car standing on the running boards. It was their responsibility to guide the driver to keep a safe distance from either side of the road and warn him of any approaching hazards we would encounter. Needless to say our journey took a while travelling at about 10 mph. However, we eventually made it home safely with no mishaps. Can you imagine attempting that these days!

Roger Savage

Wet Dreams

Having secured my first car a VW Beetle for a bargain price of £35, I was now a fully mobile seventeen-year old. The price of £35 wasn't without its problems as explained in my previous story but the coast was all clear and I was ready to hit the road.

It was the summer of 1969 and the thoughts of a motoring summer holiday were on the agenda, myself and two pals decide that a week in Devon might be the answer, we packed what we thought we would need for a week's holiday and prepared to leave Eastbourne for sunny Paignton in Devon, however before leaving we needed some words of "advice" from our parents as this was our first holiday on our own, duly advised off we set full of anticipation for the week ahead.

All was going well with the journey, progress was being made not at a fast rate the car wasn't capable of that but we were on our way.

However on the main route to Devon we came across what to us looked like a massive hill known as "Telegraph Hill" the VW wasn't the most powerful of vehicles and she struggled to make the hill in fact the only way she could make it was by my two pals getting out and pushing but eventually we reached the summit and with the sound of other motorists "encouraging" remarks ringing in our ears we were back on our way.

Paignton was now in our sights and the anticipation of what lay ahead was exhilarating, first job was to find a camp site unfortunately this was the height of the summer season and having not had the fore thought to book ahead we struggled, but what we happened upon was a stroke of luck or so we thought, the camp site aptly named "Heaven in Devon" we approached the reception office to be told yes they had one of their premier pitches available for a very reasonable rate, this didn't take long to decide yes this was for us and was shown to our pitch.

There is was nestled on the side of a slight hill with the sun shining on it perfect, we duly pitched our tent without too much difficulty and set ourselves up for the week ahead, fortunately for us the local pub "The Anchor " was a short walk away from the site so having completed day one tasks we thought that a reward of a couple of pints was in order you may recall that we were seventeen at the time but to three young strapping lads this wasn't a deterrent, into the Anchor we went and proceeded to enjoy pints of Whitbread Trophy and as luck would have it on route back to the campsite we passed a fish and chip shop, cod and chips out of the paper never tasted so good now it was time to bed down for the night.

Reading weather reports was never part of the trips preparations so when our neighbours informed us that the night ahead could be a bit damp it took us by surprise but with Whitbread Trophy and cod and chips inside us nothing was going to stop us having a good night's rest. At about two in the morning we awoke to a fine mist penetrating the tent at an increasing rate, it was now throwing it down and our tent wasn't that water proof and us and our gear were getting increasingly wet and as seasoned campers will know do not camp at the bottom of a slope as the water tends run off the slope straight through the tent.

Fortunately for us one of our near neighbours were two lads in a large "deluxe" tent that was totally water proof and they had watched with some amusement our predicament and offered us accommodation for the night and encouraging words that the weather for the rest of the week was going to be fine, so rather damp we accepted there kind offer and joined them in their tent for what hopefully was going to be a dry rest of the night, but before settling down they insisted in one final drink whilst telling tales of there "interesting careers" as grave diggers and going into some of the more unsavoury parts of their job!

Needless to say sleep didn't come easy that first night and we were glad when morning came and the sun shone and we were able to dry out and get things back in shape.

Now as the day progressed and the sun got warmer the wind direction changed and we started to realise why this particular site "Heaven in Devon" had vacancies because down the bottom of the valley was a pig farm whose healthy smell was working its way up the hill side as the temperature increased unfortunately the options available to us were limited so we decided to stick it out.

The rest of the week proceeded well and we had a good time we were however glad to get home for good night's rest in a bed and some home cooking by mum.

A bit more research and preparation wouldn't have gone amiss and it brings to mind the saying of "fail to prepare be prepared to fail" but for our two friendly grave diggers who for the rest of the week insisted on regularly inviting us over for a drink where more tales of their busy careers were told with some relish we may have slept a little more soundly in our beds.

David Burnett

Have we been drinking Sir?

Back in "the day" a traffic Policeman was very different from today's highly advanced offering that populates the sides of roads of Britain. Today they take on the shape of a big static yellow box balanced on a stalk that can process misdemeanours at the speed of light and have a fixed penalty notice on your doorstep before you arrive back home. Not so in the early 1980's. In those days these law enforcers were dressed in a smart dark blue suit displaying bold identification numbers on each shoulder and topped with a blue felt covered dome displaying a large shiny chrome badge of authority. This helmet was always precariously balanced and had a hard black leather strap that came down to the lower lip but no further. In the event of a potential arrest, these highly trained officers would stand bolt upright, hands clasped behind their back, flex slightly at the knees whilst rolling back onto their heels and almost imperceptibly move their chin in time with the immortal words "Ello, ello, ello, what do we have 'ere then?"

But, back to my story which occurred during my 'dark ages' when I was too old to skive at college and far too old, according to my father, not to have a 'proper' job. However, there was no sign of landing a 'proper' job so a toe into the murky world of double glazing was the best on offer.

ColdShield Double Glazing was the finest on the market with their 16 micron anodised aluminium frames, 'float glass' panes and meranti hardwood frames, blar blar blar! These facts had been indelibly implanted during my intensive training in Manchester where recruits were put into a room that used a series of flashing lights and spooky sounds similar to those used to successfully programme Michael Caine in the 'Ipcress files'.

Particular emphasis was given to educating us in ways of refusing to take 'No' for an answer and developing a level of persistence that exceeded all decent levels of politeness. There were only two ways to leave a potential client, either by taking an order with a deposit cheque or via a window on the end of a boot!

Anyway... on this particular occasion I can't recall how or why a glass of wine was involved. I may have been selling to an alcoholic or perhaps to someone who just couldn't listen to me any longer without taking to the bottle. Whatever the reason, I had had one small glass before leaving. Coming down the hill into Peacehaven a Policeman stepped into the road, arm raised and palm flat to my oncoming car, and which was in all other respects, the gesticulation of a Hitler salute! It always amused me that a Policeman would step purposefully into oncoming traffic and have the confidence, or foolishness to expect his powers to exceed that of King Canute, who incidentally, failed dismally to stop the tide coming in! Fortunately for him I was not drunk so with quick reactions was able to spare his life! Having passed this first test to determine the level of drunkenness, he moved slowly around the car to the driver's side and in time with the lowering of my window articulated his knees until his head was level with mine. "Good evening Officer, is there anything wrong?" I said nervously, at which point his unnaturally long proboscis moved forward into my cockpit and sniffed exaggeratedly several times. "Have we been drinking Sir" he rather condescendingly replied. "I've just had a very small glass of wine but that's all" I said. "Then I suggest that it's gone straight to your right foot wouldn't you Sir" was his reply! I'll never forget those words... whoever trained this guy must have had a very droll sense of humour. I couldn't laugh at the time for fear of imprisonment, but fortunately the Policeman seemed disinterested in taking things further and left me with nothing more than a fond memory to share with you!

Adrian Beal

CHAPTER 5 – WORKING

◆ ◆ ◆

'Healthy food consisted of anything edible'

◆ ◆ ◆

'We believed that spaghetti grew on trees'*

*Watch this Panorama programme from 1957. https://www.youtube.com/watch?v=tVo_wkxH9dU

Why didn't I listen at the briefing!

In the late 90's I was working in the specialist cheese and fine foods business and was always looking for advertorials in the trade Press. At the time an English vegetarian Parmesan cheese was being launched by Twineham Grange, a little farm based in West Sussex. I needed a story with a bit of excitement so came up with the idea of jumping out of an airplane holding a lump of this cheese! A decent photo of me freefalling with cheese in hand could lead to all sorts of potential headlines such as, "falling for cheese" or "drop into your supermarket and buy some today!"

The best thing about this idea, and the one that really drove it forward for me, is that Twineham's would pay for my tandem parachute jump and accompanying video. I told my brother of my plans and he was keen to jump with me, so off to Headcorn Sky Diving we went cheese in hand and expectations high. We both agreed that this was going to be the most exciting experience in our lives and were keen to get going. Arriving at Headcorn we were signed in (waiving all our rights in the event of death) and given a quick guided tour before being led into a meeting room.

There were about half a dozen of us and as many instructors telling us to "listen up" as they went through the safety briefing. Quite honestly I had come to do a parachute jump, not to listen to someone drone on about health and safety, I mean Blar Blar Blar! What part of "fun" was that? Eventually we were led into another room with all the "gear" laid out. God knows what it was, just a bunch of straps that Houdini would have looked good in, and several bins with orange overalls that, on reflection, looked like they had come from Guantanamo Bay. On hindsight I think that I must have missed the bin label that read "Ladies – Extra Small" so quite how I managed to squeeze into my suit I do not know and applying the harness was a masterclass in making the impossible possible! My God it was uncomfortable but I consoled myself that it wouldn't be for long and that it was much too much of a faff to change.

We were led in a line across the tarmac to the waiting plane like a string of prisoners on death row, but by now the adrenalin levels were on the rise and the excitement palpable. The engines were already running and the crew eager to throw in their human cargo before slinging it out again at 12,000 feet! No sooner than we seated the plane sped along the runway and took to the sky with its engines straining. It was a lovely sunny day and the view of the ground, through the hole in the side of the airplane where a door could have been expected, was spectacular. The Kent countryside began to shrink rapidly along with the airport buildings which stayed in sight as we circled on our upward trajectory. Ten minutes later we were informed that we were at our dropping zone and that the punter in the foremost seat was to move toward the open door and join with their respective instructor ready to bail out.

Fortunately I was third in line and had time to look over my shoulder at the elderly lady behind who had by now turned green and was clearly regretting having signed the insurance policy presented by her husband the previous day that had been accompanied by a single voucher for a "once in a lifetime experience". Had she bothered to look down before jumping, I could swear that she would have seen her husband standing by the perimeter fence, binoculars and mistress in hand!

Behind her was my brother with a fake grin on his face that certainly did not accurately reflect the thoughts running through his mind. I turned to face the front once again just in time to see the first victim exit the plane as if I was watching the final scene of "Where Eagles Dare" in which the traitor is given the choice of returning home to face the music or exiting the plane in exactly the same manner! Soon the second customer slipped away in the same fashion and it was me being summoned to the hole. I nervously stepped forward and introduced myself to the man now responsible for my life. "Listen up" he started, and this time I was all ears!

His instructions were clear, face forward and he would come for me from the back! "Ooh er missus!" Once attached to his chest I was to lift both feet, bend my knees and tuck them between his legs. I couldn't help wincing at the discomfort of my harness, particularly around the bits that were starting to tingle, but by now I was no more than an unwanted kit bag swinging from the unfortunate man. Staggering forward towards the gaping hole in the aircraft I was gripped by the deafening sound of the propeller thrashing the sky just feet away, and the rush of a hurricane that immediately gipped my skin tight suit and ripped it open from top to bottom along the straining zip and exposing my chest to the elements! "Look up" my instructor shouted, and I remembered the previous advice warning us that looking down could result in wetting oneself, whilst looking up would was no more scary than standing on the ground watching fluffy clouds go past. Good advice as it turned out! Seconds later we were gone, plummeting feet first into oblivion. The downward acceleration was impossible to describe but it bought on acute tingling of ones testicles as I was consumed with fear... Bloody hell, never before have I accelerated so quickly and for so long! It seemed to last an eternity although in reality it was probably only a few seconds of nerve jingling terror. Then came stage two. The instructor deployed a little parachute called a drogue which in turn pitched us forward to face the ground that was now rushing up to meet us. I don't recall any previous warnings about this part of the jump, but it was at this point that my face was completely remodelled on a grotesque gargoyle, and my cheeks started to flap furiously as they migrated toward my forehead. Furthermore my eye sockets loosened to a point where they seemed happy to let their charges pop out and swing freely on their respective optical cords, but fortunately neither of these things fully materialised. All of a sudden a figure darted into sight and I realised that it was the camera man keen to either capture the unusual image of a man falling to the ground holding a lump of parmesan, or if things should not work out too well, collect his payment for another snuff movie! Strangely this part of the experience became amazing. The excitement of falling toward a ground that was not materialising, the intensity of a gale force wind and a breath-taking view of Kent was awesome, but my favourite bit was always going to be when we gently glided through the air suspended by a large handkerchief... or so I thought. And then it happened, my kind instructor did something that I will always hate him for... he pulled the rip cord. All of a sudden we deaccelerated from 140 mph down to 20mph through my testicles! OMG! The pain! Imagine the G-forces of two heavy men dissipating all that energy through an ill-fitting harness where the lines of stress converged at my crotch! All I wanted was a sharp knife to cut myself free and enjoy my last few seconds in comfort, but instead my heartless instructor chose to speed our decent through a manoeuvre using central force rotation to swing us around the central axis thus spilling wind from the chute and achieving an emergency landing... what a chump! The rest of that jump has been erased from my memory, as is nature's way of dealing with such trauma, but the subsequent video showed a perfect landing, and a man still gripping a piece of cheese and swearing "bollocks to parmesan!"

Adrian Beal

CHAPTER 6 – WORKING ABROAD

◆ ◆ ◆

'Kebab was not even a word never mind a food'

◆ ◆ ◆

'Eating raw fish was called poverty not sushi'

◆ ◆ ◆

'None of us had ever heard of yogurt'

◆ ◆ ◆

'A Big Mac was what we wore when it was raining'

Grounded by Cunard

I joined the Merchant Navy in 1966 predominantly to reconnect with my French Canadian father who lived in Montreal. This I succeeded to do as I worked as a steward on Cunard cruise liners.

In 1967 I was on the Sylvania, (ironically this was the same ship that Mike Williams and his school pals sailed home from Canada on in 1959), heading back to England travelling on the St Lawrence seaway serving breakfast to a mixture of different nationalities when the ship came to a sudden halt.

It transpired that we were stuck on a sandbank between Lac St. Pierre and Trois-Rivières, Quebec, due to a fault by the pilot who was guiding us along the seaway. Sea going tugs were needed to pull the ship of the sandbank and we had to wait a couple of days for their arrival.

In the meantime the passengers were offered two options. Transfer to a Canadian Pacific liner to continue their journey to Southampton or be flown back to England. The crew had to remain on board and as it was summer it was very hot on board.

At some point we became famous with Canadian TV with

helicopters and film crews arriving. There were many photos being taken of the crew sunbathing, making merry and overall having their own little holiday.

It took a couple of days for the tugs to release the ship from the sandbank. We were towed back to Montreal to check for damage and repairs to be undertaken to the propellers. All crew had to remain on board with a lack of facilities including no showers. As my father lived in Montreal the chief steward allowed me to leave the ship and stay with him. At the time Expo 67 was on enabling me to visit the international festival and have a bit of a holiday and get paid for it.

Perry Begin

Vodka Dreams

In 1974 I was sent to Algeria to commission a new laundry.

Whilst there I was staying in what once was probably a beautiful former French hotel. Unfortunately by the time I arrived it had lost some of its appeal.

One evening after a meal I met some Russian engineers in the hotel bar. On finding out I was English they decided to befriend me (not like today) and invited me to join them in a few drinks!!! They had brought their own vodka with them and after two or three or maybe a few more! I was just slightly a bit worse for wear. I managed to find my room and my bed. At some point in the night I needed to visit the bathroom. As I walked to the bathroom, remember probably still a tad worse for wear, I recall feeling something on the floor under my feet. I did the necessary and back to bed still with that feeling underfoot.

The following morning my headache and I awoke to what looked like the wall moving. Good stuff that homemade vodka. As my eyes adjusted to the sunlight I soon realised the wall was not moving but a parade of large ants were carrying the dead cockroaches up the wall for a feast.

On looking down at the floor I could see black footprints of crushed cockroaches that I had unknowingly trodden on my visit to the loo during the night.

That day I moved to a more upmarket hotel and I have not touched vodka since.

Perry Begin

World Cup all at sea

In July 1966, the year of the World Cup as if anyone needed a reminder, I was on the Cunard ship Carmania with what turned out to be at least 100 passengers who were German and a crew made up of a lot of football mad scouse's.

We were serving lunch half way across the Atlantic, which meant our time difference with the UK was three hours behind, so at the time we were in the middle of lunch service. The tannoy system was keeping everyone up to a date with the score. When England scored, the English guests along with the crew were showing their appreciation in a vocal manner. When Germany scored it was the turn of the German passengers. My everlasting memory was watching the German passengers leaving the restaurant with their tails between their legs to cheering from those left still in the restaurant.

Perry Begin

The sink sank!

My pal Bill had a flat which he used to rent out and he asked me if I could change a work top as the previous tenants had burnt the existing one. I said no problem; I will pick one up from Magnet and fit it in no time. I picked up a cheap top and went round to the flat to replace the damaged one. Bill was not there so I cracked on and very quickly, I had the new one fitted and was marking the top to cut the hole out for the sink. I had put the masking tape on the work top and marked the four corners of the sink when Bill said, come on let's go to the crown for a liquid lunch and me being a weak person and fond of the ale agreed.

Well we got in the pub and stayed in there till it closed at three and if George the landlord wasn't going out we would had stayed later. We got back to the flat and I told Bill I would just cut the hole out for the sink as the plumber was coming to fit it on his way home. So I connected my four corners up and proceeded to cut out the hole. All done I cleaned up, put my tools away, and almost as an afterthought I decided to try the sink in the hole to make sure it fitted. I certainly didn't want the plumber moaning it was too tight. As I dropped the sink over the hole, with Bill standing there, you can imagine my horror when the new sink fell straight through the hole and onto the shelf below. I looked at Bill. Calm as anything he smiled and said "Looks like we need another work top and you better cancel the plumber."

I went back to Magnet the next day and explained what I had done and as I was a very regular customer they gave me another work top and marked it down as damaged, so I basically got it for a fiver, and refitted it this time cutting the correct size hole. The lessons learnt hear was, don't go back to work when you have been in the pub until closing time!

Jim Fell

CHAPTER 7 – SPORT

◆ ◆ ◆

'If you didn't peel potatoes you were considered lazy'

◆ ◆ ◆

'Cubed sugar was considered posh'

◆ ◆ ◆

'Indian restaurants were only found in India'

◆ ◆ ◆

'Chicken was for special occasions'

Sport and bicycles

As I got a bit older the back alley games were superseded by cricket and football in Bingham Park a ten minute walk from our house. It only took a couple of house calls whilst carrying an armful of kit to raise enough of the gang to create a team or two and go off for hours of fun. We only had to shout to Mum or Dad "we're off to the park," and away we went. Back then of course, we all had our first bikes, none of this ferrying back and forth in the car by our parents, you made your own way. Somehow we managed to carry our football or cricket kit and in the imagination of our young minds Bingham Park became our Wembley, our Lords or even an obstacle course or cycle racing track. The park was pretty much square in shape with pathways all around the perimeter, ideal for bike racing. Woe betides any dog walkers who got in our way. I also with my bike, and school satchel, became very useful to my parents for trips to the local shops one trip of which on a rainy Feb 1952 day I was told that the King had died. I can recall though that this momentous happening didn't really mean too much at the time until my parents were able to explain to a ten year old about the Monarchy.

Ray Fry

Cricket Quick heal

As Match Sec. for a local rugby club, it was my job to send out team sheets for the following weekend's matches (photocopies sent by post – this is the days before emails). I then had to take the calls from those who could not play and find replacements. The excuses for not being available to play were many and varied including one player who had forgotten (genuinely) that he was getting married on the day of the match. One of best, however, was the call from a player informing me that he could not play because he had broken his leg. I offered sympathy and told him I would, of course, arrange a replacement. He thanked me and then assured me that he would be OK for the following weekend!

Tony Uden

Little 'Hampton'

In the 1990's when I was a young Chairman of Eastbourne Cricket Club, the Saturday 2nd team were short of one player and I offered to drive to Littlehampton to make up the numbers, even if only to field. As it happened we won and our 1st team (Captained by Richard Halsall, who became England's fielding coach in 2007) playing at home lost, most unusual as they were a very good team in those days. However, on the following Tuesday at our committee meeting, as chairman I could not help saying to Richard, "Sorry about your 'little Hampton' on Saturday" which was immediately picked up by Peter Bibby our Junior's chairman, who wanted to record my comments in the minutes.

All I could say was, well he was just coming out of the showers at the time!

John Heald

Cricket Club(ing)

In the early 1990's when Sussex had a week of cricket at the Saffron's cricket ground in Eastbourne, some of the Sussex team sometimes stayed at my house, probably not for my company, but more because I have a swimming pool.

On this occasion on the Monday of a three day game Ian Gould the wicketkeeper asked if he could stay as the team were going Clubbing in Eastbourne that night and his wife said it was ok. As he was going to be back late he borrowed a key. He eventually came back at 3.20am and having lost the key knocked on my neighbour's house in error. My neighbour Cynthia answered the door in her dressing gown to which Ian asked, "Oh! Are you staying here too?"

Richard Holste

Below the belt

Being the second eldest of ten children and the eldest of five under five at the time, my childhood in the 1960s was very happy but also, in certain aspects very hard. I passed my 11 plus exam but due to the long list of expensive uniform and p/e requirements I was told in no uncertain terms that I wouldn't be going to grammar school, and instead I joined the neighbouring secondary modern school.

I was very good at most sports; football, cricket and boxing etc. playing for the school football teams and boxing for the school once a year at the Brighton Dome as well as our inter house tournaments. On the day of our school cricket trials at the age of twelve I was selected to play for the school team verses our neighbouring grammar school. The day before the game I was informed by the sports master that I would be required to wear a white shirt and long white trousers, neither of which I possessed, nor had any chance of getting as I was only allowed I pair of long trousers per year which had to be grey flannelled as per school uniform. I explained this to my sports master who said that he didn't want to lose his opening bat and would sort something out for me.

On the day of the match he produced a white shirt which was two sizes too small and a pair of whites that were at least two sizes too big however, with a few tucks and wrap overs, I padded up, opened the batting and though I say it myself, looked rather good. After a few cover drives and a few other manufactured swipes the trousers became rather loose and eventually, despite my best efforts to hold them up, dropped down onto the top of my pads and hanging over my ankles! As if this wasn't bad enough the only two pairs of underpants that I possessed were in the weekly wash and I was left red faced in all my glory to the amusement and delight of the throngs of both sets of schools supporters and teachers! The sports master raised his finger with me having made the customary 25 runs at which point you we're obliged to retire. I trudged off half holding my trousers up, and managing to maintain a huge smile.

That episode followed me and my four brothers, who attended the school after me, around for a few years with the occasional shout of "Got yer pants on today Longy?" Needless to say that they ensured that they wore underpants to school every day!

Geoff Long

Cricket, lovely cricket

T'was at Edgbaston Brum I first saw it, West Indian legends. They be, Walcott, Weeks and Worrell - the famous three. Actually, the first time I saw a first class match In Warwickshire, was when a young New Zealand fast bowler Pritchard played. He was so fast that the wicket keeper and slips were fielding halfway to the boundary! I went on to play in my youth in Brum in the Small Heath Parks league. I was usually a last minute replacement for one of the Electrical Components team, which my Dad, as the best bowler and batsman, captained. We played on a coconut matting wicket, which was alarmingly fast. It did not help that young fast bowling lads fresh from the West Indies were often in opposing teams and terrifying. Going in at eleven I could be counted on to stay there, provided I did not offer an attacking shot! As soon as I did I got bowled. Later on I starred for the third team in leafy Kenilworth Warwickshire where most of the team comprised of local rugby players, as it was a great way of getting cheap beer day and night!

Moving South, I proudly told northern mates that I was playing for Sussex, this was sort of true, as Hellingly thirds were based there! At University, I normally only watched. My less fortunate mate found himself playing against a local Yorkshire colliery team that was far too good for us. He was last man in. The local wicketkeeper advised him,

"Keep thi ed daan lad, our young quickie is a mite evil. 'E don't recognise bein' soft on't tail enders!"

The tousle headed scowling young bowler roared in. The first ball shot through my mates legs missing the wicket by a whisker and went for four byes. Now enraged, his second ball was a bouncer that nearly decapitated the number eleven! The third removed all the stumps. As my buddy trudged off, the wicketkeeper joined him and said, "Watch out for young

Fred T, he will play for England one day, I reckon!"

Also at Uni I used to watch the Roses matches between Lancashire and Yorkshire at Bramall Lane. It was there I saw two promising Yorkshire lads who came in six and seven when we weren't doing so well. One called Chris Balderstone hit an elegant fifty and went on to play for England at football too. The other less regarded youngster also hit fifty too but very slowly. His name? Geoff Boycott! Early in my teaching career I went on the cricket tours the school arranged to the West Country. These were great fun. Teams like the Fleet Air Arm plied us with crates of beer and there was competitive pub skittles in the evening. The only downside was when they were short and I had to play, usually hidden away at long on.

At one village we had to help de poo the pitch of cow dung before we played! However, it was whilst there, that my greatest cricket achievement occurred. We had two Minor County players in our side and a sprinkling of Sussex Premier League players so we weren't bad. On this occasion our fast bowler Pat had a field day and took nine of their ten wickets. Desperately keen to get a career record tenth he called in the field but instructed me to remain on the boundary. He finally roared in facing their captain and best player. I meanwhile was so keen and excited, disregarded his instructions and moved twenty odd yards in towards the wicket. Their batsmen took a huge swing; slightly miss hitting it, and the ball flew like an arrow in my direction. My whole cricketing life flashed before me. The ball seemed to float in slow motion towards me. What if I dropped it? Pat and the rest of the team would never speak to me again. The ball more or less smashed into my hands and stuck! A huge smile of relief spread over my face as I proudly marched up to our triumphant bowler. He stared in my direction and muttered, "I told you to stay on the boundary!" So much for fame!

Mike Williams

400 Not Out

I was brought up among the 'Dark Satanic Mills` of West Yorkshire in a town called Elland. This relatively small mill town sits in the Calder Valley between Huddersfield to the south, Halifax to the north and Brighouse and Leeds to the east. Going west from Elland, however, is a different proposition altogether as you soon will find yourself in the Pennine hills leading across the moors and on into the Manchester conurbation. In so many ways mine was a classic working class up-bringing amidst a classic working-class family. There was my dad, John Hedley Bottomley and more of him later, along with my mother and my elder sister.

We lived in a corner house in a long line of back-to- back-back terrace housing. Being on the end our house had a shop at the front from where my mum ran her hairdressing business. It was a lady's hairdressers and despite the many years my mum worked in this shop I'm pleased to say she never got round to calling it a `salon`. The one central theme within this down to earth, tell it as it was community was sport and that sport was cricket with the White Rose emblem sewed on jumpers and shirts and games played at every opportunity both by children in and round the houses through to the semi-professional players of the northern leagues at the Elland C.C. All this cricket and occasional football matches were played by the boys in our street and all matches were played in front of the storage garages that belonged to the saw mill that lay behind them.

Our stadium or as it was called back then our home ground was known as the GARAGES END, much thought had obviously been given to the naming rights but heaven knows who thought of putting the `END` after Garages, there must have been some deep thinkers among the citizens of South Street. We school children played cricket every minute of our spare time with all the details of tactics, technique and performance discussed endlessly among family, friends and team mates when we were all too knackered to run around anymore. After school as many as 20 children and sometimes more would organise games of cricket that often continued until it was too dark to see.

My memory now insists we also played all day on Saturdays and Sundays and in the school holidays with endless time for unlimited time-test matches. These matches went on for five or even six and seven days producing matches that also had a result and always retained the Ashes.

That love of beating the Aussies in any sport but particularly at cricket has never left me. But, to understand this story even further you also have to understand about my dad, John Hedley, and his own sporting ability. He was prolific at school sports captaining the senior cricket first team in only his third year at his senior school. He was also a prolific goal scorer for the school football first team and by the time he was 15 years old he was participating in trials at Huddersfield Town Football Club. However, it was cricket where his heart lay and he was immensely proud and honoured to be invited to Yorkshire County Cricket Club to participate in what we would call today a `development programme` but in those days as a 'trialist' young batsman.

The step up from talented junior to seasoned professional in any sport, in any age is huge and John Hedley unfortunately never quite made that step. This rejection, however, never tainted his love of playing cricket and football and he would very often join our games of cricket after work against the saw mill garages, joining in with pent up energy created from his work simply because he just loved to play and loved even more to bat.

So, readers you now have the scene set for you to understand what happens next in this memory story. Working Class Holidays: Most of the towns in West Yorkshire had different holiday weeks when the towns shut down, literally, and the population moved to the seaside for the annual holiday. The denizens of Elland were no different and usually families went to one of a number of seaside resorts. Scarborough was a favourite and Bridlington and Skegness were also popular destinations. Some even went to Blackpool, much decried as this was red rose country not really suited to holidays but more of a day out destination such as visiting the Illuminations at Blackpool.

However, my family's resort of choice was Filey and as far as John Hedley was concerned it was a choice for a very good reason and that reason was the beach. Filey had one of the best cricket beaches, if not the best, on the east coast of England! So, what makes a cricket beach. It is a beach with a big tidal spread, in other words the sea goes out a long way.

This tidal spread is fundamental as it allowed the cricketers to play on partially wet sand that does not degenerate into castle making sand! Castle-making sand makes the worst of all beach pitches as the sand is fluffy, loose textured and does not remain firm, all of which is incompatible with running around in ankle deep sand induces feelings of training to join the Royal Marines. However, slightly wet sand also allowed for flowing cricket enabling players to perfect classic cover drives, pull and cut shots all around the pitch. The essence of a beach cricket pitch, therefore, is one prepared from sand that remains firm allowing bounce and movement of the cricket ball, well in our case the tennis ball and John Hedley knew this. He knew you needed to be down on the beach as soon after the tide had retreated as far as practical. He instilled in me the need to ensure proper reconnaissance of sand conditions and preparation of tides and times before play could start or even continue on subsequent days.

All this was just some of the many life lessons he passed on to his only son and heir. If only my six year-old twin grandsons, Albert and Arthur, knew what lessons and knowledge their grandad has in store for them in the next couple of years they may well emigrate but heaven forbid, not to Australia. So, my family is now in Filey in August of the early 1960s for our week's holiday. I would have been something like eight or nine years old. This time in the 1960s was the beginning of the dominance of West Indian cricket led by the great Gary Sobers who had made 365 runs at Sabina Park in Jamaica against Pakistan in 1957/8. John Hedley spoke to me often about this innings and he arrived at the Filey Beach Ground in a mood to fill his life-long ambition of breaking Gary Sobers' world batting record. However, I get ahead of myself as there were, as you readers now know, pitch preparations to make. John Hedley, needless to say had arrived in Filey with a copy of the tide-table for the week. We checked out the weather forecast which looked glorious.

We inspected the sand on the day of our arrival finding a classic Filey pitch of hard sand slightly damp and rust coloured from the receding tide. Ominously the pitch was as flat and smooth as a pancake. John Hedley remarked as we strolled back to our self-catering flat that the pitch looked like a batsman's dream and a bowler's nightmare. The following day rose clear, bright and hot with just a slight refreshing on shore breeze. The picnic was prepared, copious amounts of liquid was poured into flasks and spare bottles together with spare clothing and towels pushed into carry bags. John Hedley and I were clearly excited and as it was the first day of the match my mother had agreed to umpire and my sister to field for some of the days play.

There was a slight problem with my sister as she claimed she did not and would not run around chasing a ball, this was something apparently that girls didn't do. Not wanting to get off on the wrong foot on the first day of the holiday John Hedley and I quickly conferred and agreed to my sister's insistence of not running about after the ball. We both agreed she would make an ideal first slip and if necessary, the batter would forego any runs that they may have been scored behind the wicket in favour of fielding the ball themselves.

The stage was now set for the big match. We had food and refreshments and half a dozen tennis balls obviously held in the pockets of my mother's dress which did give her some very weird body shapes but I digress. John Hedley marked out the pitch and from his back pocket pulled out the bails which were ceremoniously placed on top of the stumps. All that remained was the toss between the two captains. Mother had the coin and offered me the call. I was nervous as I knew from John Hedley that the pitch had moved from a batsman's dream to a batting paradise and that the first innings would prove crucial. Mother flipped the coin into the air and I called heads! The coin landed on the pitch hardly making any impression in the sand but showing a tail. John Hedley unsurprisingly opted to bat first.

At this stage I should give you readers some description of the various landmarks within the Filey ground. The on-side boundary was referred to as the promenade side. Behind the stumps was the Filey Brig end while the opposite batting position was simply known as the Arcade End; funny enough and you have probably guessed there was an arcade there. That leaves the boundary towards the sea on the leg side and this section of the ground was known as the Denmark Terrace named after the famous West Terrace stand at Headingley. It was known as such because John Hedley and bearing in mind that the distance to the boundary edge changed through the course of the match, as the tide turned, offered him the chance to hit huge sixes. If hit far enough out to sea John Hedley claimed they may well finish up in Denmark itself! He did tell me that he had achieved this feat once when he was a young teenager but couldn't tell me with any confidence how he actually knew the ball had reached Denmark so I still don't believe him.

The game was set, mother lowered her left arm and I ran in to bowl at medium pace with the intention of producing a ball with slight wobble in the air. The first ball was met in classic opening batsman's style with a very straight bat and the ball rolling straight back to the bowler. Wandering back to my mark I was pleased with a first dot ball but this unfortunately was the last dot ball I bowled for an hour and a half. By the time we broke for lunch I had figures of 22 overs for 67 runs and John Hedley had hit each of the 132 balls bowled straight along the ground usually past the bowler without offering one chance. The elder sister at first slip had done what she said she would and had not moved. Trying to remember this now I have wondered if the artist Antony Gormley had been watching the match from the promenade side and seen my sister stood perfectly still at first slip which then inspired his famous 'At Another Place' instillation on Crosby beach.

The afternoon session followed the pattern of the morning with John Hedley offering no chances to get him out. I changed from bowling medium to slow pace to my off-break finger spin. In an attempt to stop John Hedley scoring I bowled fifteen overs of flat off spin for a further 31 runs, leaving John Hedley on 96 not out at the close of play.

Back at our holiday flat I reflected on my bowling performance coming to the conclusion that in the afternoon session I had needed to give the ball more air to try and induce a false stroke from John Hedley. Although disappointed to have not claimed a wicket throughout the day I was happy just playing cricket with my dad.

Day two dawned bright and sunny with the mild on-shore breeze still blowing. Again, the family wandered down the beach to our chosen spot and set up the wicket. I knew the match was tightly poised and I needed a quick wicket if I was to stand any chance of winning. I need John Hedley back in the pavilion, well at least by the deck chairs, as soon as possible. Play resumed with my sister again at first slip and again confirming she was not going to run around after a ball. I knew I had bowled too flat the day before so I was determined to ensure I gave the ball plenty of air hoping this might just induce a false shot from John Hedley. The first ball of the day, I bounced in off of my hop and a step run up throwing the ball much higher. John Hedley had a look of confusion as the ball hit the pitch at a full length and viciously shot up at almost a 90 degree angle catching as it went his top hand that held the bat. The ball climb slightly higher still as a result of catching the top hand and flew to first slip where my sister held a superb catch right in front of her face. Pandemonium broke out. I was running down the wicket leaping into my sister's arms and that hadn't happened for a very long time, with my index finger raised screaming howzat , you're out, I've got you, on your way old man. I turned towards the umpire with the biggest grin on my face only to hear the fatal words "not out". What I screamed, it hit his hand, and he was caught! John Hedley was staring down the wicket at me and was clearly in no mood to 'walk', he just stubbornly stood there, leaning on his bat and refusing to leave the pitch. "How is he not out?" I wailed at the umpire she replied that the ball had not actually hit the batsman's hand but some form of impediment on the pitch and had gone close to the hand but no contact had been made, she assumed a small pebble or stone was the culprit. If only the DRS, Decision Review System had been invented and in operation in 1962 at Filey how things may have been so different. I was politely informed by the umpire again of the not out decision to which I respond by hissing "you are a bloody cheat". The next thing I knew mother had removed the middle stump out of the ground and had set about beating the back of my legs with said implement shouting as she went about her task, "you do not swear at anybody but particularly not your mother". Meanwhile my sister, still stood at first slip was laughing hysterically with tears rolling down her cheeks. "You can bloody stop laughing" I shouted only to be instantly pounced upon again by the stump wielding umpire intent on doing serious harm to my small and tender calf muscles. Not that I knew what a 'time out' was but at the suggestion of John Hedley a drinks break was taken to really allow all parties, i.e. me and the umpire, to calm down. I was visibly upset not only at the injustice of the umpiring decision but also at John Hedley's insistence of standing his ground and not playing the `game' and refusing to `walk' off.

It was much later in the day and when my heart rate had returned to near normal that my father informed me that there was no such rule in cricket where a batsman had to walk and anyway he claimed the ball had not hit his hand and an injustice would have occurred if he had given his wicket away in this manner. He also reminded me quietly that the umpire's decision was final and it was the decision that mattered most.

It was agreed by all parties that a swim in the North Sea would be a good idea and a way for all to calm down and allow a degree of normality to return. When I say all went for a swim you the reader will understand that this did not apply to my sister who refused on the grounds that it would mean getting her hair wet and that was a non-negotiable issue. You are right readers she was extremely difficult to understand at times and particularly so for an eight year old boy! After the swim and an early lunch play was resumed and as the day wore on the `not out` decision slowly faded into the background. I continued to bowl off spin and John Hedley continued to accumulate runs at an alarming rate including launching two massive sixes that he claimed were on their way to Denmark. By the close of play on day two John Hedley had taken his score onto 285 not out 11 runs short of a double hundred in a day and leaving him just 80 runs short of Gary Sobers world record individual test score.

Day three was deemed a rest day by John Hedley his thinking being a full day away from cricket would allow me to move on from the `not out` decision that was still simmering away. I was also informed that the match was a five day affair as we needed a day out from Filey before we left for home. Day four of the match turned into half a day as there was shopping and cleaning to do at the holiday home. My dad's holiday motto was, you can do what you like on your holidays apart from go out at washing up time! This motto needed to be loosely interpreted. I pointed out that there was no washing- up to do so I was going to the arcade. I didn't get far beyond the front door. Another life lesson John Hedley informed me. After lunch at the flat, play on day four was resumed but after about 30 minutes play in which John Hedley had added a further 20 runs to his total the heavens opened and play was abandoned for the day leaving John Hedley on 305 not out still 60 runs short of the Sobers' record.

The weather forecast and tide table were all in our favour on the final day of the match. John Hedley was pretty confident of being able to go past Gary Sobers record and I was equally confident I could ensure this target of 365 would not be reached. My plan was to slow down my over rate thus reducing the amount of time John Hedley had to score the necessary number of runs. My hop and step off-spin run up turned into three very slow hops followed by four very slow steps taking additional time for me to reach the crease before releasing the ball. John Hedley took his batting stance smiling to himself as much to say 'bless the boy for trying to stop the inevitable.' My new run up was a disaster,

I was concentrating so hard on hops and steps that I forgot to bowl properly. I was releasing balls that fell half way down the track allowing John Hedley to saunter down the wicket and hit the bowling either to Denmark or onto the promenade. My sister was still employed at first slip but disconcertingly she had now brought her book with her and was immersed in the story. I did ask why she was bothering to stand at first slip but she shrugged and claimed to be trying for an overall sun tan; something that was completely meaningless and beyond my comprehension. Eventually, well fairly soon actually John Hedley arrived at the moment having scored a single to tie the great Gary Sobers' score. As my run up had gone hay-wire I dropped another delivery short of a length which then required me to wade waist deep into the North Sea to retrieve another six moving the batsman's score onto 371 not out. Obviously being very pleased with himself John Hedley then informed me he had a new runs total target of 400, my heart sank.

As you readers can now imagine it didn't take many overs for John Hedley to move his score along and in what seemed like no time at all he was five runs short of an individual score of 400. I had by this time managed to restore a semblance of respectability to my run up and I was bowling much more accurately. With the last ball of my over I bowled a full-length delivery that pitched outside off-stump but with width allowing John Hedley to swivel and crash the ball into the promenade boundary wall. One more run for 400 I said as John Hedley walked down the wicket towards me. He looked at me and smiled before saying, "I am so proud of you, you have been bowling for five days and persevered throughout, you haven't yet battered so I now declare on 399 not out "I looked back at my dad and in a quiet voice said simply, "well played dad, fantastic innings so now it's my turn". He smiled, nodded and handed me the bat. My sister who we both had forgotten about was still stationed out on the Denmark terrace boundary. I called to her to explain what was happening and suggested she returned to first slip. She called back to say she was happy where she was and reminded me that she was still not running after stupid cricket balls. "Do you know what she is doing out there?" I asked John Hedley, "not a clue" he replied, "other than something to do with a sun tan."

Following a bit of limbering up I took my middle and leg guard and settled down to receive the first ball of my innings. Bowling wasn't really John Hedley's strong suit so I was sure that I should be able to score some runs on what was still a batter's paradise of a pitch. John Hedley steamed in bowling a loosener that flopped down well short of a length. I was onto it in a flash rotating to the leg side and catching the ball perfectly in the middle of the bat. I watched it soar out towards the Denmark terrace boundary and subconsciously noted four runs in my head. Barely had this thought left my mind when I noticed my sister sprinting at top speed towards the ball that was still in the air. I thought, "What is she doing? She isn't going to catch it; is she!" About six feet in front of her with the ball inches from the ground she dived, her full length of height stretching her right arm out in front of her to take and hold a one handed fantastic catch. Disbelief ensued. John Hedley was sprinting out towards her arms aloft shouting, "Go there my girl."

Completely mentally and physically crushed I realised I had just made a golden first ball duck, that my batting was done and I had been caught out by my sister who had hardly moved for the best part of five days. What a disaster! I had spent a week bowling at my father, who had never shown any mercy in his pursuit of Gary Sobers batting record and who then went on to score a total of 399 not out before declaring.

It was the end of a great holiday.

Post Script: I should add that this is a true story that happened 61 years ago this summer and while I may have embellished much of the detail this is simply down to an ageing memory. Yet despite this I do retain fond memories of playing cricket with my dad and this story is just one of the many occasions when I played cricket with the lovely man who was my dad.

John Bottomley

Golf on the Old Course

In June 1995, I went on holiday, with my wife Jan and our friends Pat and Sylvia Glynn, to Elie, a small town situated on the Firth of Forth approximately 10 miles or so south of St Andrews, in Scotland. The accommodation was a flat, owned by a distant relative, who I have never met. It was a two week holiday and the weather was scorching hot, every day.

Pat and I took our golf clubs and the intention was to play golf on a few days. When we played, our wives sometimes came with us and walked the course as we played, and on other occasions, we would meet them around lunchtime, when we would go somewhere for lunch. Pat had played the Old Course at St Andrews on a previous holiday in Scotland, but I had never played there and it was somewhere that I wanted to play. It is difficult to arrange a tee time there, and the system in place in was, and may still be, that you were required to telephone the club, before 10 am, the day before you wished to play, as the result of which, your name was entered into a ballot. It was then necessary to phone back after 4 pm the same day, to be told whether you had been successful, or not. We didn't have a specific day in mind, which as things turned out, was just as well.

We had arrived in Elie on a Saturday and the following day, I made the required calls to try and secure a slot for the Monday. I made two calls and both were unsuccessful. The same thing happened on the Monday and Tuesday, when I said to Pat "You try tomorrow, you may have more luck." He phoned on the Wednesday, and we had been allocated an 11 am tee time for Thursday. Jan and Sylv went with us to St Andrews, where we arrived at around 9.30 am and went somewhere for coffees, before arriving at the course at around 10.15 to 10.30.

The Open Championship was due to be played, at St Andrews,

two weeks later, and I had expected us to be given a piece of matting, from which we would have to play all our shots. However, this was not the case and we were able to play from the fairways, when we landed on them, and from all the other places, when we didn't. We had to pay our Green Fees, which were £55 each, to the Starter, who was located in a small hut adjacent to the first tee. All the 'stands' had been erected, in readiness for the Open. As the vast majority of people who will read this, will know, one of these stands runs along the right hand side of the first hole, which runs virtually parallel with the eighteenth. The stand runs most of the way down the first, to the right, as you play from the tee, towards the green. Immediately opposite the Starter's hut, was a single rail wooden fence, which there was a set of golf clubs leaning against, close by a man, dressed in golfing clothing? When we spoke to the Starter, he told us that the man was an American, who had just 'turned up' in the hope of being able to play. He asked us if the guy could play with us and we said 'Yes, no problem'. We introduced ourselves and our wives to him, and he then said that he wanted to hire a caddy. The Caddy Master's office was off to the right of the first tee, close to the end of the stand. There was a small number of Caddies, waiting to be employed and the American guy came back with one, a short while later. He introduced all of us to the caddy, and we were ready to play.

We invited the American guy to tee off first, and he hit a good shot, down the middle of the fairway. Pat followed him, doing exactly the same. I had arranged with Jan, to stand at the back of the tee and take a video of my first shot at 'the home of golf'. She stood in place ready and I swung the club. I made a reasonable contact with the ball, but sliced it way right, into the 'Stand', where it then pinged around, before flying out of the end of the 'Stand' finishing quite close to the group of Caddies. Pat said to me, "Are you going to get it?" and I said, "Not bloody likely". I placed another ball on the tee and hit it straight, and we were off on our round.

Memories dim somewhat, of even an event as auspicious as playing at St Andrews, but I do recall managing to not hit too many more slices like the first tee shot. I also remember that, not unnaturally, the course was a tough challenge. The American's caddie was brilliant with Pat and I as, in addition to helping his 'employer', he also helped us, by telling us where we needed to try and hit the ball.

Anyone who has played St Andrews, will know that most of the greens are 'doubles' and are huge, leaving handicap golfers with, on occasions, very long and undulating putts. The caddy was pointing out where we should attempt to put and several times that was nowhere near where I would have aimed, had he said nothing. Two or three times I said to him that I was going to have another putt, after we had finished the hole, and was then nowhere near the line that had been required. That was tough enough, even when managing to get it somewhere close to the correct line.

When we got to the seventeenth 'Road Hole' tee, the caddy told us where we needed to aim if we hoped to finish on the fairway, beyond the St Andrews Hotel. As on the first tee, I was the last to tee off, following good shots from both the American and Pat. For around only the second or third time, I sliced my tee shot. It curved around the end of the hotel, out of sight. The caddy said, "That'll be in the fish pond in front of the hotel, are you going to play another one?" I said "Yes," placed a ball on the tee and again sliced it, shorter than the first, but further to the right. It hit the end of the hotel, and we could hear it, bouncing around below a solid balcony wall. After a few seconds, two heads appeared, above the balcony top. They were decorators, working on the inside of the balcony. As we walked towards the hotel, one of the guys threw my ball back out onto the fairway and I eventually finished the hole with it. Pat played a really good second shot, onto the right hand edge of the green, and putted up to within inches, to almost make a birdie.

As we walked up the eighteenth fairway, there were a small number of members of the public leaning on the fence which runs along the right hand side of the hole, watching those playing, and some of them actually clapped us, as we walked past.

When our golf was finished, we said our goodbyes to the American guy, and Pat and I, both handed the Caddy a twenty pound tip, because had had been so helpful, making it an even more enjoyable experience than it might have been, had he not have helped. It was a very enjoyable experience to play the Old Course, but a tough challenge.

Paul Roberts

Crail, putting and a foot(ball)

It's the last day of our Scottish Holiday, in July 1995. On the final say of our holiday, in which my mate Pat and I had played several rounds of golf, sometimes accompanied by my wife Jan and Pat's wife Sylv, we had booked a tee time at what turned out to be a beautiful links course, at a place called Crail. Crail is located at the tip of the north coast of the Firth of Forth, known as the 'Nook of Fife,' with the Crail Golfing Society, the seventh oldest golf club in the world founded by eleven gentlemen in 1786, situated a further two miles east with fantastic view over the north sea. There are two golf courses at Crail, the original and revered Balcomie Links and since we were there, a championship course opened in 1998. Also, like Elie, it is around ten miles from St Andrews, but to the south east of it. We obviously played on the Balcomie Links.

As we stepped onto the first tee, it was another wonderful morning for playing golf. We have been to Scotland a number of times over the years, and the weather on this occasion had been exceptionally sunny and hot, not unlike the summer here in Eastbourne, in 2022, although the temperature at Crail didn't reach the dizzy heights of this year. Somewhere around the third or fourth hole of this lovely course, on a hole of which I cannot remember the par, I was faced with a very straightforward, chip and run shot, over a ridge of around eighteen inches in height, which was situated approximately ten yards or so, short of the green that we were playing to. I was around twenty yards short of the ridge. Pat was already on the green and Jan and Sylv, both well versed in the requirements to stand still and more importantly, keep quiet, were standing behind the green. I proceeded to play my shot, the kind of shot, which at the time I found relatively easy to make a good job of. In fact back then, my short game and putting was what enabled me to play the game, to a half decent level. However, when I played this particular shot, I hit an ignorant jerk; ok, not a person but one of my golfing terms for a bloody awful shot; with the club, which sent the ball scuttling along the ground ahead of me. It had travelled less than half the required distance, with just enough momentum to run up and over the face of the ridge, which was something like a three of four course high, wall covered in grass.

As I was somewhat prone to do in those days and thankfully a little less so these days, I slammed my eight iron into the turf, with the force that would have broken open a coconut or some of my toes, had they been in the 'line of fire'. As I then walked towards the green, I yanked my putter out of my bag, with enough force to almost send me off balance. I then went to smash the putter head on the turf, missing completely, the planet that we live on, and hit the outside of my right ankle, with such force that I was instantly in agonising pain. Pat, Jan and Sylv had not seen me hit my ankle, but in no time at all, it was like having a football for an ankle. It was impossible to disguise the ensuing limp and as I arrived at the green, Jan said to me, "What have you done?" to which I replied, "You really don't want to know."

How I completed that round of golf, I have no idea, but I was determined to do it, the pain and the limp, both becoming progressively more acute. We had decided before playing golf that we liked the look of the clubhouse enough, to stay and have lunch there. The views were stunning and the aroma from the kitchen was enough to encourage us to stay. Pat and I went to the bar, whilst the 'girls' sat at a table, overlooking both the course and the beautiful Firth of Forth. As we were ordering the drinks, Pat said to the barman, "Do you by any chance have a bag of ice cubes that my mate here could put on his ankle, he's injured it whilst out on the course?" The barman said, "No unfortunately I haven't, but what I do have in the freezer is a very large bag of frozen peas, which can be defrosted, as we have a meal for a large group, this evening in the clubhouse, so I can cook them from unfrozen." I then spent the lunch period, sitting with my right foot on a chair, beside the one on which I was sitting, with my entire foot covered in this huge bag of peas, suffering earache from Jan, whilst Pat and Sylv found it quite amusing.

Pat said to me that he thought I should get my ankle examined, at a hospital. The barman said that the only hospital locally, was a Cottage Hospital, in St Andrews. The barman gave us instructions of where we could find the hospital, and when we finished our lunch, we set off towards the town. We had intended going to St Andrews for a final visit, on the last afternoon of what had been a thoroughly enjoyable holiday. Pat drove, and we made it to St Andrews, but not to visit the town instead finding the hospital, with no A & E. We went inside the hospital and explained to a receptionist why we were there. She showed us to a waiting area and said "I will call a local GP, to come and examine your foot." We waited for something in excess of two hours, before what turned out to be a lady doctor arrived. She took me into a small room, where she said "I'm very sorry". I instantly stopped her and said, "I suspect you are going to apologise for us having to wait. Please don't, because when I tell you what I have done, I suspect that you may want to smack me around the head, which is probably what I deserve." When I told her the story she laughed and told me that her husband is a golfer and so she has learnt from him, how frustrating the game can be. By this time my ankle was so swollen that the doctor said that she was not going to X-Ray it, as it would all be pretty inconclusive, and to get it done at home once the swelling had gone down, considerably.

We were due to attend a BBQ, at a mate's house in Uckfield, the following evening, something which Jan was looking forward to, and my 'punishment', was to have to drive the 450 odd miles, with my ankle the size of a football and constantly throbbing with agony. Unlike today, at that time I did not have a car with automatic transmission, and so got no relief from braking. Fortunately, due to all the Advanced Level driving courses I had done in the police, I brake, probably around a quarter of the times that an average driver does, which alleviated some of the pressure on the ankle. Later on during the Friday, I had looked at my ankle, whilst back at the flat, where we were staying, and there was a perfect imprint, of the shape of the sole of my putter, which had a very shallow curve from end to end.

Paul Roberts

Little Green Man

Back in the mid 90's when the dress code was not as relaxed as it is today, on Sundays if you wanted to have a beer after your round, and didn't want to drink in the spike bar, you were expected to change to a smart jacket and tie.

On this particular Sunday I was in the car park in my Sunday best when a senior gentleman, not a member, approached me explaining he had lost his glider over the golf course and would it be ok to retrieve it. Me being a helpful person said, "No problem, I will get a buggy and we will go and look for your glider. Do you have an idea where it landed?" He had a rough idea where it was and in no time at all, we found it. It had come to rest in the top of the trees on the left hand side of the 16th fairway A rescue did not look very hopeful as it was in the top of the tree. He asked me if I had any ideas of how we are going to get it down. I suggested I go to the 16th green and get the flag stick and he could stand on the roof of the buggy and try to dislodge it. I explained I couldn't do it as I was all dressed up in my best. He said, not to worry, he would have a go. I pull the buggy up to the tree and he tried to get it down without any success. I could see he was a bit disappointed. The trouble was, he was much shorter in stature than the height of an average person. I said the only way that plane is coming down is if you can shimmy up the tree then knock it down, repeating that I can't do it because I am in my Sunday best! He gave me back the flag and started climbing up the tree from the roof of the buggy. The tree trunk however was covered in green slime. I took the flag and put it back to the 16 green and as I was heading back to the tree he shouted "I've got it." I rush back to help get him down, not looking where I was driving being more concerned that he didn't fall out the tree. I heard and felt a bump in the buggy and to my horror realised I had run over his precious glider, which was now detached from its wings. He slid down the trunk now looking like a leprechaun with all the green slime on him. I was so sorry and apologised profusely for what I had done. He, on the other hand was so happy to get his glider back, he told me not to worry! I took him back to the car park and off he went with his glider tucked under each arm and I went and had my well-earned pint (or two). Happy days!

Jim Fell

Dogging with the lady captain?

One lovely Friday evening I had an incident on the golf course with the lady captain. At the time I had two Lurchers, Dolly and Buster. I would take them on the golf course, very early in the morning, even before the greenkeepers were up, and sometimes late at night just before dusk. Peter Negus was the head greenkeeper and as the course was often closed to golfers he never minded me walking my dogs. They loved to chase the rabbits and squirrels. This particular day as was usual on a Friday, I would meet my mates in a local pub in Willingdon village for more than a few pints of the amber nectar. After consuming a good few pints and sorting the world out with all its problems, I headed home a bit unsteady on my feet. When I arrived home my 'fork and knife' was not yet back from a shopping trip to Bluewater shopping centre. Feeling somewhat happy from the ale I had consumed, I decided it would be a good idea to take my dogs for a walk on the golf course and also take a handful of golf balls and my putter. I also took my headphones and Walkman with me. I could do a bit of practicing while my dogs did their own thing, chasing rabbits.

Anyway, with my headphones safely in my ears, I walked to the 16th green. The light was fading; I looked down the fairway and never saw any golfers, all was clear. I don't know whether my eyesight was failing in general or specifically on this occasion, had been affected by the large amount of beer I had drunk earlier. No matter, I put my headphones on, scattered my golf balls on the green, and began practicing, with the sound of Johnny Cash's 'Ring of Fire' in my ears to which I was happily singing along. Suddenly I felt a heavy tap on my shoulder which almost made me wet myself! To my horror, I saw it was the lady captain. She wasted no time in giving me a piece of her mind. She asked "What are you doing...?" before she could continue I replied that I was practicing my putting. She then informed me she had been shouting for some time for me to get off the green as she was in a match.

I apologised and told her I never heard her. She then shouted, "Are you deaf?" I replied, "No, I was listening to Jonny Cash and that's why I never heard you shouting." She then looked at what I was wearing, dirty jeans with the knees out, old working boots, and a tatty shirt. I think she muttered something under her breath which, so as not to put more fuel on the fire, I wasn't going to ask her to repeat. I started picking up my golf balls to make a hasty retreat when to make things worse; my two dogs came running up the fairway. "Do those dogs belong to you?" She shouted. "No, no they are nothing to do with me" I replied as I dashed off and disappeared into the undergrowth with my dogs following. I recognised her but thankfully she never recognised me when she saw me a few days later in my golfing gear.

Jim Fell

Golf Course Vagrant

It was on a very hot summer's day in the school holidays. I was late getting home from a hard day's work to find my wife had been unable to take our dogs out for a walk. It wasn't a problem for the dogs as they don't like the hot weather. Regardless of their feelings they still needed to go for their constitution. So I had my dinner and took the dogs up on the downs. It was much cooler up there and more acceptable for the dogs. Making my way home, I decided to take a short cut down through the woods and across the golf course, coming onto the course by the sixth tee. The two dogs ran off in search of prey and I walked down by the 5th green and as it was a lovely warm summer's evening I decided to rest and lay my back against the sleepers. As I relaxed, enjoying the pleasant evening air, I looked over to the 12th fairway and saw a young woman walking in the semi-rough going up the right side of the fair way. There were 3 or 4 children with her, probably looking for golf balls. Being such a still evening I heard one on the children call out to her mum saying, "Mum, there is a tramp over there. Do you think he sleeps on the golf course?" The mother looked over not sure whether I had heard her child and said, "Shush" and "Get along." Two minutes past and my two dogs came to look for me when the same child shouted, "Look he has dogs; he is one of those begging tramps you see down the town." I laughed to myself as the woman and her children headed off up the fairway.

Jim Fell

A golfing holiday

Back in the 90's a group of Willingdon members used to and still do, have golfing breaks, the only difference being, back then most of us were in our 50's and now we are in our 70's. We were very lucky to have Snapper as out tour leader. He would enquire of us lads where we wanted to go and then, not only would he arrange the golf courses and the hotel but, would also collect our golf clubs and our luggage and fill one of his company vans. He was a truly great tour leader and organiser. Any way it was decided that this particular year we would go to Spain as we had been to Scotland 3 - 4 times, Bournemouth and Redditch just to name a few. So, good old Snapper, as in the past, sorted everything out perfectly.

Pain in the neck

Not sure but I think 20 of us were going. We were flying from Gatwick and our flight was 7.45 in the morning. Someone in the group managed to get us access to the pre-flight lounge where the food and drink were completely free. So when we got in there we duly took advantage of the free, not so much the food, but certainly the booze. We were all enjoying the pints on offer as drinking and flying were not as antisocial as it is now.

Most of us noticed a new member of the group was drinking rather large amounts of Vodka and not really joining in with the general happiness and social chat of the rest of the group. This lad was a new member to our club and had got invited by association; he will crop up later so let's call him Smurf. We arrived in Spain and the coach took us to the Hotel PYR, right on the beach, in the resort of Fuengirola. We booked in and yes, you've guessed it, carried on drinking. Unfortunately one of our group was unable to cope with the large amount of alcohol we had consumed and started to fall about. It was decided it would be better if he was taken to his room to sleep off the effects of the alcohol.

In the PYR hotel, they have two lifts one for the even floors and one for the odd floors. Well, the lads who were carrying the unfortunate person to his room weren't sure if his room was the 7th floor or the 8th floor so one sharp lad said "Let's go the 8th floor and if his room is on the 7th it will be easier to drag him down a couple of flights of stairs than it will be to carry him up two flights." So they went to the 8th floor which turned out to be an unlucky guess as his room was on the 7th floor. Rather than go back to reception and change lifts they bumped him down two flights of stairs to get to his room. They tossed him on the bed not noticing that his neck was bent against the headboard, and went back to the group.

Poor Brian woke up in the morning with a crooked neck and was unable to play golf for three days. Rather than getting sympathy from the rest of us, he was moaned at for messing the four balls up!

Pissed – Pissing - Pissed off.

On a lad's holiday, there are always pranks going on. One day, I decided it would be fun to put cling film over some of the toilets in the lad's rooms. I recruited well, an ex-captain, who we will call Dave to save any embarrassment. I got the cling film from a local store whilst Dave went about getting the room keys. He managed to get four sets so we went into the first bedroom and stretched the cling film over the toilet under the seat. Not a problem, we did the first three without a hitch. However, in the last room, we had put the cling film over the toilet and we were just about to leave when we heard the door being opened. The layout of the bathroom was the bath and shower was set back in an alcove so Dave and I jumped into the bath and pulled the shower curtain across and kept silent. The two lads who were sharing the room had popped back to get some more money. Brian said to Tonbridge, "I've got to have a wee" and he proceeded to take his relief. Brian's' eyesight and hearing were not the best because as he was weeing we could hear the urine hitting the cling film like a drum but poor Brian was completely oblivious and carried on. The time it took him seemed to go on forever. Eventually, he finished and went back to the room. Tonbridge then said he wanted to clean his teeth because could taste the garlic. He only had socks on and soon noticed how wet the floor was commenting to Brian there must be a leak and we should report it. We had better get a move on or we will get moaned at by the others waiting downstairs in the bar. Tonbridge took his socks off-put flip-flops on and they both left room. How Dave and I kept quiet behind that curtain I will never know to this day. We re-joined the group and waited for some comments in the morning but none came. One of the lads who shall remain nameless got caught short when going back to his room after the night out and it wasn't for a wee. Need I say more? He said it was total childish behaviour and would find out who was responsible. I chirped up that the same had been done in our room by my roommate had spotted it so he would take me off the list of suspects. He never did find the culprits.

Quite Alarming

The next prank revolved around an old-fashioned alarm clock, you know the one with two bells on either side of the hammer. It was decided to gaffer-tape it under the bed of Snapper, our leader, and set it for 4.00 am. The first mistake was we taped it under the wrong bed; in fact, it was his room-mates bed, Dave's. In the evening after either dinner or a night out we used to gather in the bar for a nightcap as if we hadn't had enough to drink in the previous five hours or so. This ended up with us not going to bed until well after one o'clock. Looking back, no wonder many of us failed to play reasonable golf with the amount of ale consumed on the previous evenings. On this particular night, we eventually went to be and at 4.00 pm the said alarm started ringing. Dave leaned over and thinking it was the phone, picked it up and said "Hello" in a grumpy voice. When there was no reply he slammed the handset back down.

Naturally, the ringing continued. With that, Dave grabbed the phone, pulled it away from the cables, and tossed it across the room! Of course, this did not stop the ringing. By this time Dave was getting more and more irate till Snapper said "Try looking under your bed, Dave." I understand it still took a while to silence the alarm clock. ZZZZZZZZZZZZ!

He who laughs last.......

The final thing that happed on this holiday, which would turn out to backfire on me and my poor roommate Slider, was a situation with Smurf, who I mentioned at the beginning, and his roommate who we thought had drawn the short straw. You will see why I use the word 'thought' later. We will call him the Banker to save him any embarrassment. I gave him that name because his career was in banking not wanking. Anyway, back to the story, as I said Smurf was acting very strange drinking far too much Vodka and maybe taking tablets as well. His golf was to the standard of someone who had only just started playing golf, scoring very low Stableford scores of 10 to 12 points each round, and also he was not mixing very well. We were sitting at a table talking about his very strange behaviour. The Banker, his roommate, who was sitting with us at the time, was becoming concerned about his behaviour. I jokingly told him he might wake up in the night and decide to strangle you; he seems to be out of his head. This worried the Banker and I felt a bit mean saying that so, to make amends said "Don't worry Banker, we have got three beds in our room, you can come and stay with us, thinking, of course, he would never take my offer up. Anyway, the subject changed and the conversation was forgotten. Slider and I were in our room getting showered and changed to go out for the evening. Slider had his shower and I followed. While I was washing I dropped the soap but never saw where it went. Slider had some shower gel so I used that. I got out of the shower and forgot about the bar of soap and where it had gone. I was getting dressed when the room doorbell rang and who was there but the Banker saying he was taking up the offer I had suggested earlier. Slider gave me one of those looks that cut you in half! Well, he was here now so it was too late to revoke my invitation. The Banker then happened to mention how untidy our room was, leaving money all over the place to which Slider said there are no thieves in here mate. The Banker then said he was going to have a shower and we said, ok we will see you down in the bar. He got undressed and went into the bathroom. We heard this almighty bang and the Banker moaning. Slider and I rushed to the door to see the Banker lying on the floor with the bar of soap I had dropped earlier, in his hand. Slider and I had a job to keep a concerned face on and couldn't wait to get down to the bar to tell the lads. Not very nice I know, but unbeknown to us the Banker was going to have the last laugh. We had a good night out and met for our normal nightcap. The Banker declined and went off to bed. Slider and I followed an hour or two later. As we approached our room we could hear this loud noise and being a bit tipsy it never occurred to us it could be someone snoring! That is until we opened our door. The noise was deafening. So, so loud, Slider looked at me a called me something unrepeatable.

Well, we tried to get some shut-eye but the snoring was so loud and relentless it was virtually impossible. We got up in the morning and agreed we couldn't have another night like that. So I suggested we went to bed earlier than the Banker, that way we would get to sleep first and I've heard people say you never hear snoring when you are asleep. So, there we were in the bar for our nightcap when someone said, "Right, who wants a drink, boys?" The banker said he would have one. Slider and I seized the opportunity and said we feel a bit tired so we will give it a miss. With that, the banker said "I won't have a drink either then; I'll go up with Jim and Slider. Our hearts sank deeper than the titanic. No sleep again. Slider and I jumped into bed as quickly as possible to get a head start. Neither of us could get to sleep but the Banker was quickly snoring away as soon as his head hit the pillow. After a while, we couldn't put up with his snoring anymore. I decided to take my mattress and sleep on the balcony and poor Slider had a pillow over his head. I lay down on the open balcony and was soon fast asleep only to be woken up at 4.00 am by the local dustmen!

Unfortunately, Slider and I had one more night to endure, before setting off home to good old Blighty. The Banker was quite chatty on the way to the airport, whilst poor Slider and I having suffered from sleep deprivation and could hardly stay awake. I learned that a friend in need should really be given a wide berth. Let another friend help them out. Ha, ha, what a great teacher experience is.

Jim Fell

Football Following the Blades

It's the 1974/75 football season and Sheffield United are having their best season in the First Division for many a long year. The season is coming to a close and they have the chance to qualify for European competition. Their next fixture is away at Birmingham City, a night match. I am sat with friends in the sixth form common room at school in Sheffield, most of us support United but there are one or two strange people amongst us that support the other lot from the wrong side of town. "Wouldn't it be great if we could all go and watch United tomorrow night." I can't remember who suggested this but it was followed by a chorus of "Yes, it would but how are we going to do that?" Quite quickly a plan started to emerge but it all revolved around one individual. The individual was our Head Boy, a very talented footballer who was the only one amongst us that drove a car to school courtesy of the match fee he received playing for Matlock Town in the then Northern Premier League, he was also a member of the schools Venture Scouts who owned.......... a mini bus!! The plan was gathering pace but there was one significant problem he was a Wednesday supporter! Could he be persuaded to firstly go along with the idea but more importantly persuade the Head of Venture Scouts, our History teacher, to lend us the scout mini bus for the evening? It all seemed highly unlikely. Of course he did! There wouldn't be a story if he hadn't!

So the next afternoon approximately ten of us bundled into the scouts dark green mini bus (I think some of us must have skived some lessons into the bargain) and set off on the epic journey to Birmingham. Remember this was a long time before mobile phones and satnav' or even multiple motorways. How we found the ground I don't know but we did, parking the mini bus up a side street some distance from the ground. I don't remember much of the game or even the result (0-0) but I do know that we decided to move from where we were originally stood at half time, at the same time as Nosey Williams went to the toilet. We assumed he would find us but he didn't, we didn't see him again for a very long time. The game ended and we started to make our way back to the mini bus assuming Nosey would join us there.

We got to the correct side street and walked up towards the mini bus, just one problem, the mini bus had vanished! We looked everywhere up and down the street, no mini bus! Had we got the wrong street? Of course not, how could nine of us possibly get that wrong. No, there was only one conclusion; the mini bus had been nicked! Now what? A degree of panic set in, how are we going to get back to Sheffield, how do we explain the loss of the scouts mini bus and where was Nosey Williams?

We waited and waited but no sign of him so we started to walk back towards the ground in the hope and expectation of finding a policeman, which we eventually did. He told us we had to walk to the nearest police station to report the theft and obtain a crime number. It was a long walk! We must have looked a sight as we trudged into the station and reported the theft of our mini bus. We didn't report a missing person. They weren't particularly sympathetic; probably Birmingham supporters; just took the details and told us to walk to New Street train station. As we had very little money between us we were going to have to try and blag our way on to a train to Sheffield. This seemed highly unlikely so the final course of action would have been a telephone box with calls to a number of parents who in those days would probably have told us "you got yourselves into this mess you can get yourselves out of it, you've all got a pair of legs".

So from the police station we headed back in the direction we came from which took us back past the road the minibus had been parked in. As we crossed the road one of the guys said "I'll just have a final look" and took off up the side street. What a waste of time the rest of us thought and carried on walking.

A few minutes later a breathless mate was running towards us shouting and gesticulating. "Stop, stop, it's there, it's back, they've brought it back!!" We ran, all of us, not believing it could be true, but it was. There was the mini bus and leaning nonchalantly against it was Nosey Williams! We had found both of them!

Not believing we could possibly have got the wrong street, how could we possibly have done that, we looked for the damage the thieves had caused when they stole the minibus. Strangely enough there wasn't any and eventually we all had to come to terms with the fact that we had all made a catastrophic mistake. It was very late when we finally got back to Sheffield but at least it was all of us and we were able to return the minibus and pretend that nothing had ever happened.

Footnote - I didn't really learn from this as many, many years later I 'lost' my car in Southampton after watching United again, something my then eight year old daughter has never let me forget.

Nigel Parkes

Fishing

When I was younger I was a second fix carpenter and worked on new council houses being built in Hamden Park. That is where I met Bill Snooks who was a finishing Forman on the site. His job was to snag (quality check) your work prior to you getting paid. Bill was an extremely friendly and happy go lucky lad I got on really well with him. Bill used to frequent my local pub, the Crown in Old Town where they had an extremely fast shove-halfpenny board. Bill was truly a premiership player compared to the rest of us, in fact it was like a drinks-machine to him as he was extremely hard to beat, even when he gave you a head start. Most of the time, we played for a pint.

Now bill knew I was a keen angler so he asked me "Do you ever get any bass?" I said I did get quite a few as my old mate T Pot and I target them in the summer as they were very easy to sell, especially to the Chinese who went mad for them. I told him we get £5 a lb (pound) so he said he would have one as his girlfriend Marion loved bass.

After a while I caught a 5lb bass and saved it for bill, dropping it off at his house in Bedford Well road. I never saw bill for a while and when I did he thanked me for the bass and said how he a Marion enjoyed it. No mention of money changing hands so I let it go and never said anything about it again. Well, six months passed and Bill had obviously forgotten about the free bass. He then asked me if I ever catch conger eels as Marion has got a recipe for baked conger, which she wanted to try. I did say to Bill that when we go conger bashing we usually let them go as they are not very popular and are not worth selling but, next time I go I'll get him one. Now I was still thinking about that 5lb bass he had for nothing, so when I caught a small eel about 10lbs, I put it in a damp sack for Bill. On the way home I called at Bills house and knocked on the door. Bill and Marion were out so I tied the sack to the door handle.

Now, what you need to know about eels is they can live a very long time out of the water and I hadn't killed this one. Bill came home from his mid-day drink and saw the eel. He took it into the kitchen and not really knowing what to do with it he tipped it out of the sack into the sink and turned the cold water tap on which woke the eel up at which point Marion screamed and ran out of the kitchen. By this time the eel was out of the sink and squirming around on the kitchen floor with Bill trying hard to shove it with a broom. Funny, after that Bill never asked me for any more fish, and I always wondered what happened to the eel.

Jim Fell

Rugby - It ain't half hard Mum!

My first serious introduction to the game was as a rather chubby eleven year old chosen to play a first year match against local deadly rivals Mosely Grammar. It was a lovely shambles, where thirty boys all chased the ball in one small corner of the pitch, whilst the entire senior team playing later, howled abuse and encouragement in equal measure! With two minutes to go the score was a predictable nil - nil. Then Fatty Williams inexplicably found himself with the ball. He tried to off load it, failed, and accidentally threw a dummy, bumped off another boy and was shovelled over the line for a winning try! He was hooked. After that I experienced the full range of rugby life. Injury was a big part of it all. I worked my way up from broken collar bones (playing the whole match not realising of course) up to serious stuff. Some were self-inflicted, most though were inflicted! In one case as a rather mouthy youngster, I got my nose broken in a local Kenilworth Stratford derby match. Whilst prone on the floor a fellow player urged me to avoid Leamington Hospital at all costs and go to Warwick if I wanted to survive!

Arriving there, Dr Khan offered me two options. "I can reset your nose manually now or you can come to surgery Monday". I chose immediate action which turned out to be marvellous! You wouldn't know now that my nose had been moved to the right hand side of my face by the force of the opposites props blow! I vividly remember Dr Khan issuing instructions to two strapping young nurses to "hold him down" as he scrunched my nose back into place. Terrifically painful but it worked. I learnt always to accept immediate action. I have had various broken and dislocated fingers caused by accidental contacts between me and opposition folk! Where I could not get someone to reset, is where they are still stiff. Black eyes were another frequent factor of life. It did not do a lot for my love life either! A piece of homely advice would be not to play in the notoriously brutal Sunday

Coventry Works league or accept invites to play in Sunday Welsh friendlies! The latter word was meaningless, for if it moved they kicked it, including you!

You meet some really interesting characters on your journeys. One famous ref called Quittenden on seeing me rolling in agony after being kicked in a private place, advised "don't rub 'em, count 'em!"

A later English international second row I played with for South Warwickshire was very mild mannered until provoked. He also had a speech impediment. On being messed about frequently by an opposition player in the line out, he announced he was "getting weally cwoss"! I tried to forewarn the opposition player that he could be really hard, but the player just continued to hassle him. Five minutes later he was stretched out cold on the pitch! "I weally did not want to do that!" He muttered.

Playing his last match before emigrating to Canada, I had the good fortune to play against the legendary Peter Jackson. As young and fit as I was, he went past me, as if I was standing still!

I went to some interesting places too. Stoop Memorial and Northampton grounds were huge and tiring, but it was worth it to meet some top players. Mind you, smaller places were more fun. Kenilworth played Burton if only for the after match experience. You bathed individually in steaming hot beer barrels and had marvellous beer tastings.

Going on tour in the Northeast always needed to include Blaydon. All of their players seem to be the same smallish size. However they could drink you under the table with ease. Kuwait rugby introduced you to the concrete pitch experience, whilst playing in Abu Dhabi showed you what it was like to play in five star luxury on lush grass pitches with fine dining afterwards.

Socially the game offers a whole range of good memories. Seven's tournaments at Twickenham used to be picnic heaven. International matches in Paris; I think I remember fondly, though not always clearly! I recall being chased by a group of very irate Basques who wrongly thought we were after their daughter. Tours to the Rex Hotel in Whitley Bay were legendary with up to seven rugby clubs there at the same time, heavy drinking guaranteed. To sum up, I pass on the words of my old school song about rugby.

'Often times defeat is splendid, victory may still be shame. Luck is good, the prize is present, but the glory's in the game.'

Mike Williams

TT Races

The Isle of Man is famous all around the world for the TT Races. Held in the first week of June I saw my first TT race aged just 6 months, in the year Geoff Duke became the first rider to lap the TT course at an average speed of 100 mph, and never missed a race until I was 22 and working in the UK. TT week was always half term for schools because with the road circuit closed pupils couldn't get there or back. My youth was a time of the John Surtees, Giacomo Agostini, Geoff Duke and Mike Hailwood battles across the madness which is the Mountain Circuit. From the age of 16 you can apply to be sworn in as a marshal. You are effectively a temporary special police constable. That was me, every year marshalling at the races. Best view but a bit dangerous on occasions.

Mike Hailwood's battles with Agostini are legendary events and I always watched the leaders from my marshalling point at Braddan Bridge.

Braddan Bridge is a bridge over the now disused railway line. It's an 'S' bend taken after a flat out ½ mile from Quarter Bridge. Even in those days Hailwood was doing close to 150mph when approaching the bend.

You need to realise that a road circuit is what it says on the tin. Public roads closed for those nutters to try not to mutilate their bodies against a house, tree, telephone box or telegraph pole.

Braddan Bridge has a large oak tree which forms a natural roundabout at the left and right turn junction. (background in the photo), Riders are to turn left at this point or have an intimate knowledge of the tree or the wall of the bridge. Along flies Hailwood and shortly before the corner when he eventually decides to break he decides he can't make the corner and he chooses to lay the bike on its side rather than hit the tree head-on.

Both he and the bike fly past us up the slip road and I along with two other highly trained marshals (really?) run after him. Well, far from him being pleased that he had escaped serious injury or that we were there to check on his wellbeing he 'f....d' his way back to his feet and, as we must, we checked he was OK. He continued to berate us as if we had run out into the highway and made him fall off. He rode past us many times more without mishap and I guess his outburst was understandable.

MR MEL LOCKETT

Champions don't do failure.

John Court

CHAPTER 8 - MARRIAGE

◆ ◆ ◆

'Cooking outside was called camping'

◆ ◆ ◆

'Spam fritters were a staple food'

◆ ◆ ◆

'We ate what mum made for our dinner or we ate nothing at all'

Getting married abroad

In 1966 I got engaged to Elke, an Austrian girl. That same year, I had a sabbatical leave from my company to take part in an economic project in South America. On my return a year later, I was offered a job to continue my career in West Africa, to begin with in Lagos, Nigeria and subsequently in Ghana. I said that I was engaged and didn't feel that I could desert my fiancé for another 18 months so 'Would they give me time to get married' No problem they said – 'how much time do you need?' A couple of months should do it, I said and this was agreed. At this time, both my future wife (working as an assistant language teacher in St Albans) and I were lacking residency qualifications and it transpired that the only solution to getting married quickly was to travel to Vienna, where we were duly married at the state registry office on September 26th 1967.

At least, I assume we were properly married, my 'O' level German being well short of fluency at that time. I do know that the registrar referred to me as Philip Huff Bal (to rhyme with 'pal'). Our honeymoon was spent driving back to the UK where, on contacting my company, I was told that Colonel Ojukwu, leader of the Biafrans (the breakaway Eastern province of Nigeria) was marching towards Lagos. The company was at that point evacuating wives and children from Nigeria so they said that there was no way that I could travel to Lagos for the time being. However, a week later, Col Ojukwu was duly repulsed by 'the gallant Federal troops' and I was told that I could now go to Lagos but my wife would have to wait until things had definitely settled down. A good start to our marriage! She was eventually able to join me 6 weeks later.

An interesting little episode – I was met at the airport by the local sales manager who told me: 'You've come at a good time. A Biafran plane was shot down here last night!' Not a reassuring start to my time in West Africa but later at a party, I mentioned this to someone. He said, 'Oh no, there's no way they could have shot it down, it must have run out of petrol!' Adventurous times with a night curfew.

One of my tasks as Lagos Area Sales Manager for Nigerian Breweries (a partnership between Unilever and Heineken) was to travel out to Lagos Airport every Friday morning to see the airport commandant, who would sign for 5,000 crates of beer to be sent out to 'the gallant federal troops' fighting in Eastern Nigeria. No doubt this gave them a suitable fillip of Dutch courage. A small role I played in helping the federal government to win the war.

Hugh Ball

(or is it Philip Huff Bal?)

A honeymoon distraction

My first wife and I got married on Wednesday 11th March 1970. We chose a midweek wedding as at the time I was playing football for Tonbridge FC and I only wanted to miss one game. After the wedding, having already hired a Mini, we drove to our honeymoon destination, where we were booked in for a week. I am not sure how long the tin cans remained attached to the rear bumper but they were not there when we arrived at the Smugglers Inn in Mevagissey.

Having spent the first few days sightseeing and doing things that most couples do on honeymoon, I noticed in a local newspaper that Brighton were playing Torquay Utd at Plainmoor (the home of Torquay) on the Saturday. I suggested to my new bride that it would be a good idea if we went and saw the game. It involved a 200 mile round trip across Dartmoor. It was March, snow was on the ground and it was bitterly cold, and of course still being in love with me, she agreed. Despite there being 4,600 fans at the game (Plainmoor is such a big stadium) it seemed like we were the only ones there. There was absolutely no atmosphere at all. It finished 0 - 0 and it was probably the worst game I'd ever seen. After the match we drove back to our base, tired, cold and hungry.

Ok, I know what you are thinking - what a selfish bastard - well you have to remember that I was 23 and my bride was 18 and we were very much in love. If you are also thinking this marriage will not last two minutes, I can tell you it lasted twenty nine years. Having enjoyed the remainder of our honeymoon it was time to make our way home to our flat in Tunbridge Wells.

As we approached Crowborough (8 miles from home) I noticed that we were very low on petrol and therefore pulled into a local petrol station. We rustled together the grand sum of three shillings which was the total amount of money we had in the world. We were able to purchase half a gallon of petrol for two shillings and sixpence or half a crown as it was known then (12.5p) which was sufficient to get us home. Those were the days!

Roger Savage

Rocky Times Travelogue

Back in 1978 I was going through a particularly rocky time in my marriage to my first wife Simone. After a while it was obvious that things were not going to improve, hence Simone moved out and divorce followed. I then threw myself into work and didn't take any holiday for almost a year. This came to light when the workshop foreman informed me that I had four weeks holiday to use up and was forced to take these weeks off with immediate effect. We needed some time apart so when Monday came I realised I had been presented with an ideal opportunity. I had to find something to occupy the next four weeks.

I hastily packed a bag, headed straight into town and obtained a one year passport which in those days was far simpler than things are now. I headed down to Dover, pre Tunnel days, with no intention of taking my car across but to use either my thumb or public transport for the next few weeks.
After much searching I found a spot to leave my car on a wide road heading out of town. I purchased my foot passenger ticket and soon I was on my way.

At this point I thought I ought to let someone in my family know where I had gone and when they might see me again, no mobiles in those days. As luck would have it I got chatting to a young guy who whenever he finished work by midday would get a ticket to France and back without getting off. This enabled him to make use of the duty free system which sadly no longer exists. I gave him my brother's phone number and he happily put them in the picture, even though they were convinced it was a wind up until I failed to materialise after a few days.

Once on the other side it was time to test what response I might get trying to hitch a lift to Paris. It took a while but eventually I was picked up by what I assumed to be a father and his daughter of school age who didn't stop trying out her English on me, which was far better than sitting in silence. From memory I would put this lift at about 25 miles which I was more than happy with. It took a while for the next lift to arrive but when it did it was well worth the wait. It was a French guy who had lived in Soho for a few years and spoke perfect English. He assumed immediately that I was heading for Paris and informed me that he was heading for the south of France and would happily drop me off on the périphérique, that's fine with me. After about an hour he suggested we call in at one of the many Mammouth superstores where the food was good and reasonably priced. I said I would pay for the lunches which I felt was the least I could do but he wasn't having any of it and paid for our food.

As the journey progressed he asked what my plans were when I reached Paris. I hadn't actually given it much thought but said I wanted to find a not too expensive hotel which was fairly central for sightseeing if possible. He then asked what I wanted to see and for no obvious reason I blurted out the Arc de Triomphe. We eventually reached Paris at which point his generosity amazed me. He took me to an area of Paris which he said I should return to as it fitted the criteria I had given and then dropped me off at the Arc de Triomphe, a great human being.

I found a hotel which definitely fitted my remit and one that I returned to several years later with my current wife Jane. After a snooze in the hotel I set off to see the Paris nightlife which I found to be relaxed and very much to my liking as I wandered around enjoying a couple of beers as I went.

A while later I reached Le Pigalle, the area where you will find the Moulin Rouge and many other 'interesting places', as those of you that have been there will know.

I shortly came across a bar which had some decent music

playing and gave me the impression of being a bit livelier than most places I had passed and decided to call in. On entering I made a beeline for the bar, purchased a beer and was soon accompanied by a couple of 'ladies' who worked in the bar, but not behind it, nor collecting glasses. It was quite possibly the quickest pint I've ever drunk before I hastily departed.

My next stop was to find a nice restaurant which I soon did and found that French cooking soon lived up to its reputation. I had a fillet steak in a Roquefort cheese sauce which in those days didn't seem to appear in your average English restaurant menus, mouth-watering! Over the next few days I think I covered most of the well-known attractions and fell in love with the cafe culture in Paris and probably the rest of France. It was however, time to move on. Once I've decided where to go?

Decision made I left Paris and headed east towards Rheims, the unofficial capital of the champagne region, or so I was told. For a reason I can't really explain I couldn't connect with Rheims other than assuming it fell well short of Paris. Admittedly it has a very impressive cathedral but everything else seemed to centre on the champagne industry, a drink which I have always considered ludicrously overrated, Philistine I hear you cry. I would willingly swap a bottle of champers for a good pint of Harvey's.

Onto the next port of call which was a visit to Luxembourg which was not too far away. As always the first thing to do was find a hotel and drop my travel bag off leaving me free to head out for a leisurely evening stroll and see what was on offer. Although not Paris, for obvious reasons, I liked what I saw and became aware of a few things that I would be visiting the following day. I finished my evening with a pizza and a couple of beers looking forward to what tomorrow would bring.

I wasn't disappointed, the first thing which I had noticed was that the city is clean, nice looking and quite high which from various points give impressive views, much of which is the rural surroundings which include the Ardennes Forest to the north. Like all European cities there is always the obligatory cathedral which all seem to be called Notre Dame.

I spent a good few hours generally strolling about picking up places such as the Grand Ducal Palace and a walk across the Pont Adolphe, a high stone arch bridge across a valley with superb views.

After lunch I headed for the old part of town to visit the Bock casements which were brought to my attention the previous evening. This cave system was built in the mid 1600's and was reckoned to be the most impregnable defence system in Europe at that time. The caves were dug down to a depth of 40 metres down into a sheer cliff face with positions facing outwards where canons could be placed at several levels. The caves were approximately 40 kilometres in length but have now been reduced to about half of that length and are open to the public. These caves at the time could house thousands of troops, horses and all facilities to survive for periods of time. In my opinion this was probably the most impressive place I visited during this mini tour. I have to admit I have visited a website to remind me of the scale of the Bock Casements.

It was now about 5 or 6 o'clock and after a day walking I was feeling a bit weary so it was time to head back to my hotel for a short nap and then find somewhere for a bite to eat and a beer or two. On route back to the hotel I noticed a burger restaurant with a bar above which fitted my needs perfectly. The burger was well above the normal standard served up at fast food outlets which raised my hopes for a decent pint upstairs, I was not to be disappointed. The bar was empty with the exception of two very attractive barmaids who served up a very nice pint.

After a nanosecond of choosing where to sit I decided on the nearest bar stool where I could converse with the barmaids who were as pleasant as they were easy on the eye. It transpired that they were both from Iceland and like I, had been touring about, they liked Luxemburg and have been there ever since. My intention of having a couple of beers soon disappeared, from about 8 o'clock I was on free beers and burgers. As impressive as the Bock Casements were, they had now slipped into second place in my Grand Duchy highlights. 11 o'clock came and the girl's informed me that the evening was at an end as they had to close up and I must leave. But wait, all was not lost, they asked me to wait outside and they would be out in about 30 minutes, and then we could go clubbing!

Whilst I would dearly love to report that I had gone clubbing and fulfilled the many fantasies that were in my head at the time but alas it was not to be. Long before the 30 minutes were up I realised that after 5 or 6 hours of drinking pints of beer, mostly free, I was in no fit state to walk let alone go clubbing. Pussy I can hear you thinking, all I can say to that is Meow! The cure however was beginning to work.

After a morning farewell stroll around Luxembourg it was time to move on. As I write this I'm filled with very fond memories of this city with its relaxed feel, the picturesque views and especially the Bock Casements. Of course there is also the memory of spending a pleasant evening in the company of a pair of generous and very attractive young ladies from Iceland.

Time to check my itinerary which tends to be made up as I travel along, Decision made and it's off to Bonn, in those days the capital of West Germany, which in about 12 years or so would revert back to Berlin after the removal of the Berlin wall and the reunification of East and West Germany. Although not a large Capital City for a country the size of Germany it appeared to have more than enough culture for the likes of me. They even have a place called the Kunstmuseum which I found disconcerting until I realised I had misread its name. They also have a Women's Museum which I think is commendable. I would however like to think they have a corner to one side honouring the men whose inventions have made women's lives easier, e.g. the electric steam iron etc.. Ouch ladies, I'm only kidding!

I was wandering around when I came across the home of the composer Beethoven, a small house with the exterior painted, as all of the houses were, in pastel colours which certainly got my vote. Once inside it still surprised me with its size, much smaller than I would have expected for someone so revered. In one room there was a small piano on which we must assume he composed most of his works.

(Was it here that he composed his one and only opera Fidelio, which I saw at Glyndebourne only in 2021? I'm no opera aficionado but thanks Beety for making it your last. The most memorable part of the evening for me was at the interval when Pete Moulding's wife Jan gave me a nudge and said "Do you know what's going on, I've been asleep.")

I found a calmness about Bonn which made it so easy to stroll about without needing to hunt out the visitor attractions, just follow your nose and see what's around the corner. I'm a bit of a fan of seeing rivers such as the Rhine which passes through Bonn. I think it's easy to romanticise about them which unfortunately cannot be said about our own River Thames. The evening was pretty much a continuation of the day with the inclusion of a few drinks and hopefully a nice meal. Strangely to this day I can only remember my wonderful steak with Roquefort sauce in Paris and 2 or 3 burgers through the evening in Luxembourg, opposite ends of the culinary spectrum.

The next day I intended moving on but decided to have a last look around the town during which I called into a few shops just out of curiosity. One shop which drew me in was an impressive looking record shop where I lost all sense of time. On returning to the hotel I was immediately informed that I had missed my checking out time and would have to pay for another night. Briefly I considered this an affront and was ready for a heated debate until I came to my senses. Why get into an argument about staying in Bonn for another 24 hours, (make that 22,) don't be late checking out tomorrow. Another day was spent at walking pace, bumped into Beethoven again in the form of a bronze statue, had lunch in a large park beside the Rhine and went one better with a short trip on the river itself. Although I didn't realise it then it was to be the nearest thing I had known to retirement. Another quiet evening followed and tomorrow it would be time to move on.

The last point of call took me into Belgium and a couple of days in Brussels. This was the only destination on this trip to which I had previously been. On that occasion it was to be my base whilst attending an organised weekend which took in a trip to the Weiss Beer Festival, my current visit would be teetotal in comparison.

On arrival it was the usual grab a bite to eat, find a reasonably priced room and head out for a stroll to see what was about. Purely by accident I came across the 'Mannekin Pis', which I'm sure many of you will know of even if you haven't seen it. It is a small bronze statue of a young boy urinating into a fountain. Being cynical I'm not sure it deserves the acclaim it receives. That evening it was the usual stroll, a few beers followed by something to eat. For the meal I went to a pedestrianised area which I had passed earlier which had several restaurants to choose from. From memory the meal was good as were a couple of glasses of wine which accompanied it.

The following day I decided to take a trip to the Atomium, the large atom-like structure built for the 1958 World's Fair.

Until now my assumption was that it was just a structure, not realising that you can go inside it and travel amongst the spheres via lift and escalators. Each sphere had its own display, many of which I think were science based. The view from the top sphere is superb, across Brussels and for miles beyond. There was one other view which in years to come would become headline news for the wrong reasons. Adjacent to the Atomium was the Heysel Stadium where numerous lives were lost at a football match between Liverpool and Juventus.

The last day has arrived and it's back to Dover to catch the ferry. Once off the ferry it was the lengthy hike back to my car which was almost on the outskirts of town. On arrival at my car there were numerous parking tickets tied to my door handle plus a note requesting that when I return could I go straight to Ladywell (I think) police station. Once there I questioned what was wrong with my parking as you could drive a tank past my car and there were no 'No Parking' signs. What I then learnt,

please take note, was that if there are double white lines in the centre of the road you cannot park at the adjacent kerb, no matter how wide the road is. For this I was fined and given points on my licence.
Welcome home!!

Alan Elms

CHAPTER 9 – FOOD

❖ ❖ ❖

'Seaweed was not considered a food'

❖ ❖ ❖

'Fish did not have fingers'

❖ ❖ ❖

'Sugar had a good press and was called white gold'

❖ ❖ ❖

'Surprisingly Muesli was readily available.
It was called cattle food'

Food glorious food

The youngsters of today have no idea what they missed out on! For a start, faggot and pea shops that abounded all round Birmingham. The basic contents of innards may not appeal so much these days, but it was delicious hot food served in very generous portions! Also in Brum, Fleur-de-lis steak and kidney pies that were made near Warwick, but served everywhere with superb gravy mixed with wonderfully crunchy chips. A plus was to add the tomato or brown sauce made locally in the Birmingham suburb of Aston, called HP sauce. In Sheffield , before they demolished the old quarter near the University, there used to be a marvellous group of very basic, very cheap food places run by old ladies. Here you could get huge portions of various roasts served out of large pans. The Shepherd's pie was to die for, when smothered in loads of Hammonds Chop Sauce freely provided!

Meals in restaurants were rare in our family. Trips to Balti houses in Balsall Heath did happen, but whilst we loved the decorative Balti dishes themselves, the content could be suspect. It was best not to examine the meat bones too closely, as stories regarding the use of dog and cat meat, if very unfairly, did abound!

Meals out at relatives were more the norm, if very samey. My grandmother always produced the same Sunday afternoon salad, served in the front room, the only time you were allowed in there. It comprised one wafer thin slice of ham, one slice of chicken from Sat lunch leftovers, one piece of cheddar cheese, one tomato, half a boiled egg, beetroot slices, one slice of white bread, one radish and some tired lettuce leaves and the saving grace, ancient salad cream which drowned out the other tastes. Auntie Alice, who lived in a railway carriage at the bottom of a nursery, produced much better stuff. Amazing rabbit stew, wonderful bread and butter pudding and banana cake. Auntie Phyll spent many years in the Far East, so you had to get used to things like what we termed Nasty Goreng and curries that burnt your mouth! Mum was a master stew maker. It was so solid that you could tip the plate without it spilling! Mind you, you had to like weird veg. The only thing I could not take was tripe and onions. The chewy texture just turned me off.

My favourite meal was the easiest and cheapest to do. Toast roasted on the open hearth covered with dripping left over from a beef Sunday lunch! Simply outstanding.

I save the worst to last. Like most of my contemporaries I suffered badly at the hands of school meals! Sweets were particularly dreadful. I recall especially, concrete which in another life had been called Shortbread, but which by the time we got it either crushed your teeth or became lethal ammunition against fellow diners! Frogspawn, which I think was tapioca or something similar, tasted revolting. Semolina was at least edible, especially if you whipped in strawberry jam to make a multi coloured mess. The king dessert of distress always remained what could be done to rice pudding to ensure, no one in their right mind would touch it! I was told by my grandchildren, that it remains the same to this day!

Mike Williams

CHAPTER 10 - SHORTS

◆ ◆ ◆

'Pineapples came in chunks in a tin'

◆ ◆ ◆

'Water came out of a tap' If someone had suggested bottling it and charging more than petrol they would have been a laughing stock.

◆ ◆ ◆

'Fast food was Fish & Chips'

◆ ◆ ◆

'The one thing we never had on the table was – ELBOWS'

Firsts

1. First haircut: Boy's haircuts sixpence 3d. (1p)

2. First car: A second-hand Ford Popular - £280.00. This car was followed a few years later in 1965 by a bright new red Triumph Herald convertible. I had been ogling this for some time in a showroom which I passed every day on my way to work in my first job in Manor Park, East London. The indicated price was - £750.00. I was very disappointed to hear the salesman say as we walked round the car – "Aha, this model has disk brakes that will be an extra £57.00. You're joking I thought – extra for brakes!!

3. First salary: £850.00 a year, as a Unilever management trainee.

4. First house: £7,000.00. This was relatively expensive in 1968 and bought a nice three-bedroom bungalow opposite Cheltenham racecourse.

5. First joke: When the army acquired land from my father's farm in a compulsory purchase for the construction of a prisoner of war camp in 1942, anyone visiting our farm had to pass through a military checkpoint. A cattle lorry driver coming to pick up calves from our farm told us of the following exchange when to he arrived at the checkpoint:

Soldier: "Where are you going?"

Driver: "Balls."

Soldier: "Don't be cheeky!"

6. First tennis: On 2 tennis courts built by the Americans for their soldiers at the POW camp. I was probably 8 years old when I first played (which means that I have been playing the game for some 72 years).

Hugh Ball

Halcyon Days

The early 60's were the time when school finished at the end of July and we were left to entertain ourselves for the next six weeks, apart from a week when you were either taken away for a week holiday or spent a week visiting different relatives. The sun seemed to shine from 7 in the morning until 9 at night all throughout the summer holidays (perhaps that's just wishful thinking).

The days would follow a similar pattern. Once the parents had gone off to work a further couple of hours were spent resting in bed for the exertions that were to come.

First off a bowl of cereal, make a jam (or something similar) sandwich to sustain you. Meet up with the rest of the chaps and patrol the back alleys for bottles to take back to the off licence. Stash any bottles away safely for later then a trip over to the golf course for a golf ball hunt. Sell any balls found to the players. Once we had funds, back to stash of bottles to cash them in at the off licence, all in exchange for a pack of five cigarettes. Then on to sitting in our camp with sandwich and enjoy a smoke after lunch. A trip was sometimes called for around the local building sites or road work to try to identify if there was enough rope to nick later to make a swing in the trees. Some days were spent sitting around the pond hoping to catch the many fish that we were sure were in there but we only seemed to see one or two. Back home for dinner and then back on the road again to see what other mischief we could get up to.

Bob Smith

Stammer

After my basic training at Beverley barracks, East Yorkshire Regiment in 1956 I was posted to the 1st Battalion in Osnabruck, Northern Germany. One day watching one of our drill sergeants, who had a famous stammer, putting a platoon of recruits through their paces, right wheel, left wheel when suddenly the group were heading straight for the M/T shed walls. The drill sergeant bellowed "Platoon, aboutttttttttttttttttttttt, for f...s sake stop" and hearing this we could not contain our laughter. With that our Sergeant turned on us and shouted "Why don't all of you fffffff..k off. So I have a stammer, WHAT'S YOUR FFFFFFF.....G EXCUSE'

John Heald

My own Little Red Riding Hood

I was probably about 6 years old. Our cat came into the room and, comparing it with my grandma's slightly wizened face, I announced that 'grandma looks like pussy'. My grandma remarked: "That's interesting. Let's take a photograph of the cat and myself and see if you can tell the difference." "Oh, that's easy, I said. Pussy's got 4 legs." Always knew I had a logical brain.

Hugh Ball

Bygone trades

I have fond memories of the various trades that were around in the 1940s/50s. One is of a family friend, Harold who often babysat for us with his wife Mena on Wednesday nights when my parents Fish & Chip shop was closed and they had a chance to go dancing.

Harold also worked for Ringtons Tea and would deliver tea to our door probably once a fortnight. He would turn up at our Fish & Chip shop in his Ringtons Tea Pony & Trap.

Mum would make a fuss of him, give him a cup of tea (No coffee then, not even instant) and, if I recall correctly my dad also gave him a free Fish and Chip lunch.

We also had, albeit infrequently, visits from French Onion sellers riding on bicycles laden with onions.

Our greengroceries were delivered by Dawson's horse and cart similar to the photo and yes, like the Bill Prest story of growing up in East Yorkshire, the horse was called Dobbin.

And finally a guy once turned up with a bicycle which turned a grindstone offering to sharpen your knives. You never see this trade today but it is still prevalent in India and Asia.

My dad being a fish fryer and needing sharp knives duly handed his precious tools over to the man.

The result was a flaming row with my dad refusing to pay him for "Ruining my bloody knives."

LIFE'S A GRIND to the Briton who coupled the rear wheel of his bicycle to a grindstone with a belt, and travels the countryside sharpening housewives' cutlery. The bicycle lets him cover a wide area and his own sturdy legs provide all the power he needs

Mel Lockett

Humpty Dumpty

When I was a Gas Fitter I was late one morning. When the foreman asked why I arrived late I replied, "I got up early enough but tripped, fell backwards, developed a humpty back and rocked myself back to sleep."
An appropriate bollocking followed.

Reg Cork

The End

About the Editor

Mel Lockett was born in Sheffield nine months after the outbreak of World War 2. Mel never excelled at exams and thus missed out on getting the best from his school education. However, an apprenticeship in one of Sheffield's largest Forge and Engineering companies started him on a varied career through several levels of supervisory, management and directorships in heavy engineering, shipbuilding, offshore marine and mining equipment manufacture culminating in a £4.6m Management Buy Out, (MBO) in 1996. Finally, he moved into manufacturing consultancy with his business, MCCR & Associates becoming registered with the DTI as a 'Centre of Expertise in Manufacturing' and through his associates helped over 200 companies improve their businesses profitability.

On retirement, he held several positions at Eyemouth Golf Club in south east Scotland including a 2½ year stint as club captain.

On completion of his tenure in 2016 he decided to write his autobiography entitled 'He Changes the Rules'* mainly for his children, grandchildren and future descendants. He moved to Eastbourne in the summer of 2018 with his wife Cath and joined Willingdon Golf Club in September that year.

Mel Lockett books published on Amazon Kindle.
1. He Changes the Rules - autobiography - Mel Lockett

2. What's Your Story? - Charity book 1 - Mel Lockett

3. Road to Jahra - novel - Mike Williams

4. The Fables of Wilkinson Belweather – A children's book - Leonard (Jack) McKenzie

5. When I was Young - charity book 2 - Mel Lockett

MR MEL LOCKETT

Printed in Great Britain
by Amazon